TEMPLES
SACRED SYMBOLISM, ETERNAL BLESSINGS

TEMPLES

SACRED SYMBOLISM, ETERNAL BLESSINGS

DAVID J. RIDGES

CFI
An Imprint of Cedar Fort, Inc.
Springville, Utah

ISBN 13: 978-1-4621-1507-5

Published by CFI, an imprint of Cedar Fort, Inc.
2373 W. 700 S., Springville, UT 84663
Distributed by Cedar Fort, Inc., www.cedarfort.com

Library of Congress Control Number: 2014945650

Cover design by Shawnda T. Craig
Cover design © 2014 Lyle Mortimer
Edited and typeset by Kevin Haws

Printed in the United States of America

10 9 8 7 6 5 4 3 2

Printed on acid-free paper

Dedication

To my eternal companion, Janette,
who loves temples too.

Contents

Introduction

Our modern temples are, in effect, Heavenly Father's classrooms for teaching His plan of salvation to us, especially during endowment and sealing sessions. Particularly during the endowment, He uses much symbolism. The symbolism during this sacred teaching is infinitely deep, meaning that there is no end to what we can be taught by the Holy Ghost. That is one reason why, even though the words used are the same each time, we can be taught different things, according to our needs at that particular time.

Likewise, going back to Old Testament times, we see that the Lord used plan of salvation symbolism as He instructed Moses on the layout and construction of the Tabernacle and the rites and sacrifices to be used in association with it. We can study the use of symbolism there and thus become better at recognizing it in our modern temple worship. We will trust that endowed members will recognize the similarities. We will be careful not to discuss things outside of the temple that should only be discussed in the temple.

We will also point out some architectural symbolism, especially that of the Salt Lake Temple. Everything about the temple serves to impress our minds and hearts with the Father's "great plan of happiness" (Alma 42:8), allowing it to be an ever-present force and influence in our lives.

Sources

- *Old Testament Student Manual,* Genesis—2 Samuel, (1981), Institutes of Religion.
- *Eternal Marriage Student Manual,* Institutes of Religion, Religion 234 and 235, 2003.
- *Encyclopedia of Mormonism,* ed. Daniel H. Ludlow, 5 vols. (1992).
- *Doctrines of the Gospel Student Manual,* 1986 edition, used by Institutes of Religion.
- *Mormon Doctrine,* Second Edition, (Bookcraft, Salt Lake City, 1979).
- *Discourses of Brigham Young,* (Deseret Book: 1977).
- *New International Version of the Bible,* Zondervan Publishing House, Grand Rapids Michigan (1984).
- *Endowed from on High: Temple Preparation Seminar Teacher's Manual,* The Church of Jesus Christ of Latter-day Saints, (1995).

Chapter 1: God's Use of Symbolism in Teaching

T he temple is the Father's classroom for teaching His children the plan of salvation. Several years ago in a meeting in one of the temples, we were told that much of what is presented in the endowment is symbolic. In the years since, that simple statement has strongly influenced my understanding and appreciation of the endowment.

President Boyd K. Packer once said, "It may help you to realize that the teaching in the temples is done in symbolic fashion" (*Eternal Marriage Student Manual*, 319).

Elder John A. Widtsoe taught, "We live in a world of symbols. No man or woman can come out of the temple endowed as he should be, unless he has seen, beyond the symbol, the mighty realities for which the symbols stand" ("Temple Worship," 62, quoted in the *Eternal Marriage Student Manual*, 314).

The following quote emphasizes the role of symbolism as used in the temple to teach eternal truths.

The most sacred symbolic teachings on earth are received in the temple. In a symbolic way, the teachings and rituals of the temple take us on an upward journey toward eternal life, ending with a symbolic entrance into the presence of God. The characters depicted, the physical setting, the clothing worn, the signs given, and all the events covered in the temple are symbolic. When they are understood, they will help each person recognize truth and grow spiritually. (*Endowed from on High: Temple Preparation Seminar Teacher's Manual* [1995], 23)

The scriptures are filled with symbolism. God's creations themselves are symbolic. They clearly teach that He exists and bear witness of His love for us. "All things are created and made to bear record of me" (Moses 6:63). Temples are symbolic in design and structure. Just looking at them inspires mankind to look upward to heaven for guidance and purpose.

The power of symbolism lies in the fact that it is infinitely deep. It allows a multitude of teaching levels, depending on our readiness, current needs, and stage of life. In the temple, the Holy Ghost can respond to each person individually, even with all in attendance hearing the same exact words of the endowment, as revealed to the Prophet Joseph Smith. The same thing happens when we read the scriptures. The words and symbolism are the same each time, but our needs vary with time, age, and circumstances. Recognizing the fact that symbolism is a major component of the teaching done in temples, especially in the endowment, is vital for maximum value each time we attend.

The Temple Is a "House of Learning"

In the dedicatory prayer for the Kirtland Temple, Joseph Smith referred to it as "a house of learning" (D&C 109:8). Indeed, modern temples are the Lord's classrooms in which worthy members of the Church are taught the "great plan of happiness" (Alma 42:8). Temple ordinances and instruction provide knowledge, strength, and protection in mortality as we pursue the path to exaltation in celestial glory. Sacred covenants are part of this instruction. Elder Russell M. Nelson said, "A covenant made with God should be regarded not as restrictive but as protective. Covenants with Him protect us from danger" (*Ensign*, October 2010, 49).

By the way, have you noticed that covenants apply only to entrance into the celestial kingdom, which is the presence of the Father and the Son? No covenants or ordinances are required for entrance to terrestrial or telestial glory. And, in fact, the ordinances of baptism and confirmation are required for entrance into celestial glory (except for children who die before the age of accountability—see D&C 132:10). Thus, the ordinances of the temple, except for baptism for the dead and confirmation for them, pertain to attaining exaltation for us and for those for whom we serve as proxies.

Ordinances in the gospel can be defined as priesthood rites and ceremonies that accomplish spiritual goals. These include blessings of babies, baptism, confirmation, sacrament, administering to the sick, blessings of counsel and comfort, setting apart to Church callings, ordaining to priesthood offices, dedicating of graves, and the higher ordinances received in the temple: washings, anointings, the endowment, and celestial marriage.

As previously stated, the Father's desire and plan is for us to become like He is. The endowment is His way of teaching us about the plan and empowering us to successfully continue progressing through its various stages. As we do so, we gain the required growth and development necessary to become gods. Very briefly, the stages of progression of the plan of salvation consist of:

- Premortality
- The Creation
- The Fall of Adam and Eve
- The Atonement of Jesus Christ
- Mortal life
- The postmortal spirit world
- The Millennium
- Resurrection
- The Final Judgment Day
- Three degrees of glory, sons of perdition, exaltation
- Becoming gods and having eternal families

The covenants and ordinances we make in endowments and sealings enable us, through our faithfulness, to complete the divine course and indeed become like our Father.

President Gordon B. Hinckley said that the temple "becomes a school of instruction in the sweet and sacred things of God. Here we have outlined the plan of a loving

Father in behalf of His sons and daughters of all generations. Here we have sketched before us the odyssey of man's eternal journey from premortal existence through this life to the life beyond. Great fundamental and basic truths are taught with clarity and simplicity well within the understanding of all who hear" ("The Salt Lake Temple," *Ensign*, March 1993, 5–6).

Many years ago, Elder John A. Widtsoe of the Quorum of the Twelve stated,

> The temple endowment relates the story of man's eternal journey; sets forth the conditions upon which progress in the eternal journey depends; requires covenants or agreements of those participating, to accept and use the laws of progress; gives tests by which our willingness and fitness for righteousness may be known, and finally points out the ultimate destiny of those who love truth and live by it. (Program of the Church of Jesus Christ of Latter-day Saints, 178; also quoted in the Institutes of Religion *Eternal Marriage Student Manual*, 315)

Concerning the type of covenants made during the temple endowment, Elder James E. Talmage taught,

> The ordinances of the endowment embody certain obligations on the part of the individual, such as covenant and promise to observe the law of strict virtue and chastity, to be charitable, benevolent, tolerant and pure; to devote both talent and material means

to the spread of truth and the uplifting of the race; to maintain devotion to the cause of truth; and to seek in every way to contribute to the great preparation that the earth may be made ready to receive her King,—the Lord Jesus Christ. With the taking of each covenant and the assuming of each obligation a promised blessing is pronounced, contingent upon the faithful observance of the conditions. (*The House of the Lord*, revised ed. [1976], 84)

The word *endowment* means "gift." The temple endowment is a gift of knowledge and power from God to His children. Speaking of the blessings of the temple, Elder M. Russell Ballard taught, "The endowment is literally a gift of power" ("Let Us Think Straight," Brigham Young University Education Week devotional, Aug. 20, 2013, 7).

The endowment is vital for us. Joseph Smith said, "You need an endowment, brethren, in order that you may be prepared and able to overcome all things" (*History of the Church,* 2:309).

Everything about our temples is designed to promote feelings of reverence and anticipation to learn more about God and our relationship with Him. Even as we walk onto the temple grounds, we feel the symbolic representations of the beauties of heaven in the landscaping surrounding the temple. When we look at a temple, our eye is naturally drawn upward to the sky and, symbolically, to heaven. The heart is drawn away from the world and into the celestial realm.

Architectural Symbolism

President Boyd K. Packer taught that temples themselves are symbols.

> The temple itself becomes a symbol. If you have seen one of the temples at night, fully lighted, you know what an impressive sight that can be. The house of the Lord, bathed in light, standing out in the darkness, becomes symbolic of the power and the inspiration of the gospel of Jesus Christ standing as a beacon in a world that sinks ever further into spiritual darkness. (*The Holy Temple*, 1982, 7)

The Salt Lake Temple is an excellent example of symbolism incorporated into the design and function of a temple. It is a reminder that if we train ourselves to look for symbolism, we will be amply rewarded by what we find. Such training to look for symbolism can extend to our study of the scriptures as well as to our temple worship.

Architectural Symbolism–Salt Lake Temple

1. **Angel Moroni**: Symbolizes the Restoration of the gospel and continued revelation from heaven to man on earth.
2. **The Three East Towers**: Symbolize the Melchizedek Priesthood. They are six feet taller (210 feet) than the west towers (204 feet), symbolizing that the Melchizedek Priesthood presides over the Church in spiritual matters and all other concerns. They also represent the President of the Church and his two

counselors, and also represent the stake president and his two counselors on a local level.

3. **The Three West Towers**: Represent the Aaronic Priesthood, working under the direction of the Melchizedek Priesthood. They also represent the Presiding Bishopric of the Church, and also the bishop and his two counselors at the local level.

4. **The Twelve Little Towers on Each of the Six Main Towers**: Represent the Twelve Apostles, who support the First Presidency and all the work of the Church. These sets of twelve towers also represent the high council at the local level.

5. **The Four Corner Main Towers**: Represent the four corners of the earth, symbolizing that missionary work must take the gospel to the four corners of the earth.

6. **Cloud Stones with Rays of Light Piercing Through, East Center Tower**: Represent the gospel being taken to the four corners of the earth and the gospel light piercing through superstition and spiritual darkness.

7. **The Big Dipper, West Center Tower**: Represents that those who are lost may look to the priesthood for guidance and thus find their way back to God.

8. **The Dedicatory Inscription** ("Holiness to the Lord" below the cloud-stones with rays of light on the east center tower): Represents the reality of the establishment of God's kingdom on earth with the temple as His personal sanctuary, where heaven and earth are joined and where man on earth can commune with God in heaven and vice versa.

9. **The All-Seeing Eye, East Center Tower** (set in the next window that is below the dedicatory inscription): Represents that God can always see you and knows when you need His help. It also represents that God can see all the good works and evil deeds of man.

10. **The Clasped Hand, East Center Tower** (set in the next window down): Represents the hand of fellowship of one member to another within the gospel.

11. **Star Stones** (around the top of the temple): Represent the heavens and that man on earth must keep his eye toward heaven and God's help to him.

12. **Sun Stones, Moon Stones, Earth Stones** (in descending order on various facades of the temple): Represent the various kingdoms of glory in the next life. Earth stones (near ground level) represent telestial glory. Moon stones represent terrestrial glory. Sun stones represent celestial glory. They are to be read from the ground up, symbolizing that man on earth must look heavenward. They also represent the various stages of the earth's progress, eventually becoming a celestial planet.

Note: I was told during a personal tour of the Salt Lake Temple, conducted by the temple engineer, that the ground upon which the structure is located was uniquely prepared by the Lord for such a heavy building. The ground immediately around Temple Square could not have supported the weight and the temple would have leaned or sunk somewhat.

Sources

- A talk by Harold B. Lee, parts of which I recorded while on my mission in Austria, 1960–63.
- A personal tour with four others of the entire building, conducted by the temple engineer while we were Church history curriculum writers for the seminaries of the Church in 1975.
- *The Salt Lake Temple: A Monument to a People.* 1983, University Services, Incorporated, Salt Lake City, Utah, First Edition.

Chapter 2: Eternal Blessings

The mirrors in the sealing rooms of temples are symbolic of seeing down the ages into eternity. Everything about temples and temple worship is designed to remind us that we are eternal beings. If we keep this vital perspective in mind, it influences every aspect of our lives here on earth. It gives confidence and meaning and power to endure. It increases our ability to appreciate beauty and the worth of souls, the power to resist temptation, the capacity to set worthy goals, and the places our mortal energies can best be expended. The ordinances and covenants of the temple assure the highest degree of satisfaction and happiness throughout eternity.

The endowment is absoutely required for exaltation, as is celestial marriage. Brigham Young made this observation as he dedicated the cornerstone of the Salt Lake Temple,

> Your endowment is, to receive all those ordinances in
> the house of the Lord, which are necessary for you,
> after you have departed this life, to enable you to walk
> back to the presence of the Father, passing the angels
> who stand as sentinels, being enabled to give them the

key words, the signs and tokens, pertaining to the holy Priesthood, and gain your eternal exaltation in spite of earth and hell. (*Discourses of Brigham Young* [Deseret Book: 1977], 416)

In the dedicatory prayer for the Kirtland Temple, given to the Prophet Joseph Smith by revelation, there are a great many blessings mentioned as to the benefits of attending the temple. Some of these are available to us right here in mortality and others are blessings to be attained and received in eternity.

Section 109 of the Doctrine and Covenants contains the complete text of the inspired Kirtland Temple dedicatory prayer given on Sunday, March 27, 1836. Using this section as a source, we will first list our responsibilities to qualify for the blessings of temple attendance. Then we will list several blessings mentioned by the Lord for temple attendance.

Our Responsibilities

1. Keep the commandments (verse 3)
2. Seek to gain faith (verse 7)
3. Teach each other (verse 7)
4. Study out of the best books (verse 7)
5. Build temples (verse 8)
6. Be worthy of entering into the Lord's temple (verse 20)
7. Come to the temple with a calm, reverent attitude (verse 21)

Blessings of Temple Attendance

- Being in the presence of the Savior on certain occasions (verse 5)
- Receive divine help (verse 10)
- Have God's promises fulfilled in our lives (verse 11)
- Feel the glory of God around us (verse 12)
- Feel the power of God (verse 13)
- Have testimony borne to our souls that it is a holy house of God (verse 13)
- Be taught from on high (verse 14)
- Receive a fulness of the Holy Ghost (verse 15)
- Be organized as part of God's kingdom (verse 15)
- Be prepared to receive everything we need for exaltation (verse 15)
- Be allowed to speedily repent (verse 21)
- Receive all the promised blessings from God (verse 21)
- Be armed with power after temple visits (verse 22)
- Have the name of the Father upon us (verse 22)
- Have the protection and help of angels (verse 22)
- Be strengthened for spreading the gospel (verse 23)
- Have our testimonies strengthened (verse 23)
- Be established and strengthened for eternity (verse 24)
- Be strengthened to ultimately triumph over all our enemies (verse 25)
- Be strengthened to ultimately triumph over all forms of wickedness (verse 26)
- Have the Lord on our side in all things (verse 28)
- Be strengthened to do the Lord's work (verse 33)
- Receive mercy from Jehovah and have our sins blotted out (verse 34)

- Obtain power from on high (verse 35)
- Be fortified against the extra troubles of the last days (verse 38)
- Be gathered to Christ and have joy in living (verse 39)
- Be prepared to survive the burning at the Second Coming (verse 46)
- Have our hearts softened (verse 56)
- Have help in overcoming prejudices (verse 56)
- Gain favor in the sight of others (verse 56)
- Be better able to radiate the gospel to others (verse 57)
- Be part of the majestic last days' gathering of Israel (verse 59)
- Be prepared to meet the coming Savior at the time of the Second Coming (verse 75)
- Be made clean and pure and clothed with robes of righteousness in the presence of God (verse 76)
- Receive celestial exaltation (verse 76)
- Ultimately receive eternal joy (verse 76)
- Be desirous to sing with the angels of heaven in praising the Lord (verse 79)
- Be prepared to shout aloud for joy when the time comes to receive salvation (verse 80)

It is clear from the above list that the blessings of temple attendance are rich and abundant. We are indeed "endowed" with knowledge, power, divine aid, protection, testimony, and a host of other perspectives and blessings through our participation in temple ordinances. The "riches of eternity" (D&C 67:2) are placed at our fingertips in the temple.

The Meaning of Eternal Blessings

Because we are mortals and the immediacy of daily routines and concerns often focuses our minds on the mundane things of life, we can sometimes fail to grasp the significance and meaning of the phrase *eternal blessings*.

One of the things temple worship does for us, and to us, is keep an eternal perspective in the front of our minds. This can wonderfully affect our lives. The prospect of eternal blessings in future exaltation can add much richness to daily living. Such perspective can bring light and hope, even in dismal circumstances, and can make pleasant living conditions all the more wonderful. Among the righteous Nephites who lived in constant danger and warfare, with Captain Moroni at the helm of their armies, we are told that "there never was a happier time" (Alma 50:22–23).

Some members of the Church do not understand much about the meaning of *eternal blessings*. It is, at best, a hazy concept somewhere in the far distant future that is probably worth striving for. In reality, it is a very specific doctrinal reality. It is to live—as much as possible—the lifestyle that our Heavenly Father has now.

Over numerous years of teaching adult religion classes for the Church Educational System, I found it interesting, at the end of a class discussion about the plan of salvation, to point to a drawing of the celestial kingdom on the chalkboard, point to the highest degree of glory in that kingdom, and then turn to the class and ask, "What now?"

Typically, few students came up with the answer. It appears that we need to do better at relating the ordinances and covenants made during endowments and sealings with the eternal blessings and benefits of exaltation in the celestial kingdom. Covenants made in temples and kept in daily living lead to eternal blessings. Those who attain exaltation in celestial glory become gods. They enjoy the highest satisfaction and joy in the universe.

A revelation in the Doctrine and Covenants clearly states the requirements for and the blessings of exaltation. I will include notes and commentary for these verses of scripture, using bold for emphasis.

D&C 132:19–21

19 And again, verily I say unto you, **if** a man **marry** a wife **by my word**, which is **my law**, and **by the new and everlasting covenant** [*if the marriage is performed according to the law of celestial marriage*], **and it is sealed** unto them **by the Holy Spirit of promise** [*and it is ratified by the Holy Ghost*], **by him who is anointed** [*by an authorized priesthood holder*], **unto whom I have appointed this power and the keys of this priesthood** [*who has the authority to seal on earth and in heaven*]; and it shall be said unto them—Ye shall come forth in the first resurrection [*by basic definition, "first resurrection" means those who enter "celestial glory"*]; and if it be after the first resurrection, in the next resurrection [*no matter when you are resurrected*]; and **shall inherit thrones, kingdoms, principalities**, and **powers, dominions,**

all heights and depths [*these are all terms which refer to those who become gods*]—**then shall it be written in the Lamb's Book of Life** [*the record in heaven in which the names of the exalted are written—compare with D&C 88:2, Revelation 3:5; see also Bible Dictionary "Book of Life"*], **that he shall commit no murder whereby to shed innocent blood** [*the sin against the Holy Ghost— see verse 27; in other words, if he does not commit an unpardonable sin, and deeply and sincerely repents of all other sins he commits*], and **if ye abide in my covenant** [*if you keep the law of celestial marriage and all the commandments, which includes repenting from your sins*], **and commit no murder whereby to shed innocent blood, it shall be done unto them in all things** [*all the promises of celestial marriage and exaltation will be given them*] **whatsoever my servant** [*authorized priesthood holder*] **hath put upon them** [*through authorized priesthood ordinances*]**, in time, and through all eternity**; and **shall be of full force when they are out of the world**; and **they shall pass by the angels, and the gods**, which are set there [*celestial glory is not intruded upon by unauthorized entry of evil or people who are not qualified to be there*], **to their exaltation and glory in all things**, as hath been sealed upon their heads, which glory shall be **a fulness** [*exaltation, the Father's lifestyle*] and **a continuation of the seeds** [*powers of procreation*] **forever and ever** [*having spirit children and living in the family unit forever*].

20 **Then shall they** [*the husband and wife*] **be gods**, because they have no end [*among other things, no end of having children*]; therefore shall they be from everlasting to everlasting [*will be doing the same thing the Father does*], because they continue; then shall they [*the husband and wife*] be above all, because all things are subject unto them. **Then shall they be gods**, because they [*the husband and wife*] have all power, and the angels are subject unto them.

Bruce R. McConkie explained verse 20, above, as follows (bold added for emphasis):

If righteous men have power through the gospel and its crowning ordinance of celestial marriage to become kings and priests to rule in exaltation forever, it follows that the women by their side (without whom they cannot attain exaltation) will be queens and priestesses. (Rev. 1:6; 5:10.) Exaltation grows out of the eternal union of a man and his wife. Of those whose marriage endures in eternity, the Lord says, "Then shall they be gods" (D. & C. 132:20); that is, **each of them, the man and the woman, will be a god. As such they will rule over their dominions forever.** (*Mormon Doctrine*, 613)

Verse 21, next, teaches clearly that celestial marriage is essential for exaltation.

21 Verily, verily, I say unto you, **except ye abide** [*keep*] **my law** [*the law of celestial* marriage] **ye cannot attain to this glory** [*becoming gods, exaltation*].

In Summary

The eternal blessings attainable only through making and keeping covenants entered into in the temples, including the endowment and the sealing ordinances, are no doubt far beyond our greatest imagination in scope, satisfaction, joy, and happiness. The warmth of family ties and the sociality with other exalted beings of like values and perspectives will be most enjoyable. Joseph Smith hinted that this sociality will indeed be wonderful!

> D&C 130:2
>
> 2 And that same sociality which exists among us here will exist among us there, only it will be coupled with eternal glory, which glory we do not now enjoy.

Among the great eternal blessings made available to us through faithful temple attendance and covenant keeping are the following.

- We will live in our own family unit forever, having been sealed for time and eternity. The love between spouses will know no limits and will last forever. Both husband and wife will be perfectly loveable and the love that brought them together in mortality will exceed all earthly expectation and hope.
- We will enjoy eternal association with our own mortal children who are worthy as they too become gods and create and populate their own worlds.
- We will be heavenly parents, as our heavenly parents are now. (See "The Family: A Proclamation to the World," September 23, 1995.)

- We will have spirit children (ibid.).
- We will create our own worlds and send our spirit children to them.
- We will use the same plan of salvation for our own spirit children as is now being used for us when we give them the opportunity to become like we will be (exalted). Years ago, the First Presidency explained that "only resurrected and glorified beings can become parents of spirit offspring. Only such exalted souls have reached maturity in the appointed course of eternal life; and the spirits born to them in the eternal worlds will pass in due sequence through the several stages or estates by which the glorified parents have attained exaltation" (1916 First Presidency Statement, *Improvement Era*, August 1916, 942).

By the way, *eternal life* is a term often used in the scriptures for "exaltation." Have you noticed that covenants pertain only to celestial glory?

Chapter 3: Temple Worship in the Days of Adam and Eve

When I served as a stake president, I often told members who were going to the temple for the first time to take out their endowments that it would be helpful if they considered the endowment and special temple clothing they would wear to be ancient, going back to the time of the Old Testament. With this in mind, they would feel a wonderful link to the past and a kinship with the faithful Saints of past dispensations.

I also suggested that it would be helpful for them to read and study parts of the Pearl of Great Price (especially Moses, chapters 1–4 and chapter 5, verses 1–11, as well as Abraham, chapters 4–5) as they prepared for the experience in the temple.

Elder Bruce R. McConkie taught that temples and temple ordinances go back to the time of Adam: "From the days of Adam to the present, whenever the Lord has had a people on earth, temples and temple ordinances have been a crowning feature of their worship. 'My people are always commanded to build' temples, the Lord says, 'for the glory, honor, and endowment' of all the saints (D&C 124:39–40)" (*Mormon Doctrine*, Second Edition [1979], 780).

It can be helpful for those going through the temple for the first time, as well as for veteran temple-goers, to understand that Adam and Eve were not primitive in mind and thought. They were highly intelligent and no doubt among the greatest of the "noble and great ones" among the Father's spirit children seen by Abraham in vision (Abraham 3:22).

After the Fall, they had children. They taught them to read and write, and a "book of remembrance" was kept among them (Abraham 6:5–6). Modern scripture teaches us that Adam had been taught the gospel, baptized, received the gift of the Holy Ghost, and ordained a high priest in the Melchizedek Priesthood (Moses 6:51–68). We have no doubt that Eve, his eternal companion, had likewise been taught the gospel, baptized, and given the gift of the Holy Ghost, and thus stood by his side in all things.

They were no doubt chosen and foreordained to be our "first parents" (1 Nephi 5:11) because of their greatness in premortality. Brigham Young taught that God knew that they would fulfill the necessary role of bringing about the Fall: "The Lord knew they would do this, and he had designed [*planned*] that they should" (*Discourses of Brigham Young*, 103).

Eve Made an Intentional Choice

A serious problem with the world's view of Eve is that she is almost universally viewed as the one who caused all of the misery among the inhabitants of the earth. According to this view, her partaking of the forbidden fruit was the genesis of all the woes and physical misery we encounter in mortality.

This is a tragic false doctrine. The belief that she was naïve and completely gullible and thus deceived by Satan, with dire consequences for us all, is absolutely contrary to the principles of accountability, as taught in the scriptures. Accountability and resulting punishment require that a person be taught, be capable of understanding, and be free to exercise personal agency. The worldview of Eve violates all of these eternal laws.

In *The Encyclopedia of Mormonism*, we read the correct doctrine about Eve's role in bringing about the Fall. It is clear that we owe her a huge debt of gratitude (bold added for emphasis).

> Satan was present to tempt Adam and Eve, much as he would try to thwart others in their divine missions: "and he sought also to beguile Eve, for he knew not the mind of God, wherefore he sought to destroy the world" (Moses 4:6). **Eve faced the choice between selfish ease and unselfishly facing tribulation and death** (*Evidences and Reconciliations* by John A. Widt-soe, 193). As befit her calling, she realized that there was no other way and **deliberately chose mortal life**

so as to further the purpose of God and bring children into the world. (*The Encyclopedia of Mormonism,* "Eve")

Elder John A. Widtsoe explained how Adam and Eve could have made an intelligent and informed choice even though they had been "innocent" in the Garden of Eden.

> Such was the problem before our first parents: to remain forever at selfish ease in the Garden of Eden, or to face unselfishly tribulation and death, in bringing to pass the purposes of the Lord for a host of waiting spirit children. They chose the latter. This they did with open eyes and minds as to consequences. The memory of their former estates [*including their premortal spirit existence*] may have been dimmed, but the gospel had been taught them during their sojourn [*stay*] in the Garden of Eden. . . . The choice that they made raises Adam and Even to preeminence among all who have come on earth. (*Evidences and Reconciliations,* 193–194)

The Apostle Paul says Eve was deceived (1 Timothy 2:14). But the above quotes indicate that, in the big sense concerning the necessity for and purposes of the Fall, she was not deceived. We will probably have to wait until we get a chance to talk to Eve herself, perhaps during the Millennium, for the complete account. If we listen carefully to what she said, as the account is given in holy places, we are reminded that she asked important and intelligent questions before partaking of the fruit, and responded with unselfishness.

Yet, there could be many ways in which she was deceived. Perhaps in the sense of not believing that mortality would be so difficult at times. Perhaps she had no idea what it would be like to care for twenty or thirty sick children when they all had the flu! Maybe she was deceived into thinking that old age with its attendant pains and disabilities would not be all that difficult.

Actually, she couldn't have understood these physical struggles because she had no basis on which to judge, as she and her husband were not yet mortal, even though they had physical bodies at this point. Suffice it to say that in the vital issue of whether or not to partake of the fruit, she was not deceived.

A Snake or the Devil Himself?

Many wonder if it was a serpent—the devil himself— or Lucifer in the form of a snake who tempted Eve. The answer is given in the heading to Genesis, chapter 3, in our LDS edition of the Bible. It says, "The Serpent (Lucifer) deceives Eve."

It was Lucifer himself. In scriptural symbolism, Satan is often depicted as a serpent, representing the sly, slithering, lowdown, subtle, and cunning ways he employs in his attempts to deceive us and lead us away from the ways of our Father in Heaven.

Satan has been referred to by many names in the scriptures. For example:

Revelation 12:7–9 (emphasis added)

7 And there was war in heaven: Michael and his angels fought against the **dragon**; and the **dragon** fought and his angels,

8 And prevailed not; neither was their place found any more in heaven.

9 And the great **dragon** was cast out, that **old serpent**, called the **Devil**, and **Satan**, which deceiveth the whole world: he was cast out into the earth, and his angels were cast out with him.

D&C 76:26 (emphasis added)

26 And was called **Perdition**, for the heavens wept over him—he was **Lucifer**, a son of the morning.

Adam and Eve "Fell Forward"

It is sometimes said that Adam and Eve "fell forward" rather than "fell down." In other words, the Fall was good! In partaking of the fruit of the tree of knowledge of good and evil (Moses 3:17; 4:6–12), they advanced the cause of mankind, and Eve led out in so doing. Adam was wise enough to follow. The Book of Mormon is clear in teaching that the Fall was good.

2 Nephi 2:22–25 (emphasis added)

22 And now, behold, **if Adam had not transgressed** he would not have fallen, but he would have remained in the garden of Eden. And all things which were created must have remained in the same state in which

they were after they were created; and they must have remained forever, and had no end.

23 And they would have had **no children**; wherefore they would have remained in a state of innocence, having **no joy**, for they knew no misery; doing **no good**, for they knew **no sin**.

24 But behold, **all things have been done in the wisdom of him who knoweth all things** [*it was all done according to God's plan*].

25 Adam fell that men might be; and men are, that they might have joy.

Brigham Young taught clearly that the Fall of Adam and Eve was good and according to God's plan. It was not a mistake or a surprise turn of events, as is commonly taught and believed.

> Did they [*Adam and Eve*] come out in direct opposition to God and to his government? No. But they transgressed a command of the Lord, and through that transgression sin came into the world. The Lord knew they would do this, and he had designed [*planned*] that they should. (*Discourses of Brigham Young*, 103; also quoted in the *Doctrines of the Gospel Student Manual*, 1986 ed., 21)

The Difference between Transgression and Sin

In the context of the Fall, there is a difference between *transgression* and *sin*. *Transgression* is the violation of a natural law that leads to a given consequence and is neither morally right nor wrong. It just is. Examples would include the law of gravity (such as trying to jump a fence but not jumping high enough to clear it), laws of chemistry (such as spilling acid on a surface and leaving it scarred), the laws of physics (running over a nail in the road and getting a flat tire), and so forth.

Sin is evil. It is the knowing violation of the moral commandments of God. Examples include lying, cheating, stealing, murder, adultery, abuse, and so on. They are all sins because they are the violation of the laws of righteousness.

Adam and Eve transgressed the law of remaining in the Garden of Eden as beings with physical bodies that were not yet mortal. It was not a sin. Partaking of the fruit caused the bodies created for them to become mortal and, as a consequence, they could no longer remain in the Garden. It was good. It was progress in the Father's plan for all of us. Joseph Fielding Smith taught,

> What did Adam do? The very thing the Lord wanted him to do; and I hate to hear anybody call it a sin, for it wasn't a sin. . . . I see a great difference between transgressing the law and committing a sin. (*Charge to Religious Educators*, 124; also quoted in the *Doctrines of the Gospel Student Manual*, 2000 edition, 20)

Chapter 4: Plan of Salvation Symbolism in Ancient Worship

For us today, it can be helpful to study plan of salvation symbolism that was present in ancient worship. It can greatly increase our understanding of such symbolism in our temple worship today. We will begin this part of our study with the Tabernacle used anciently by the children of Israel. It was basically a portable temple. You may be surprised at how similar much of what the Lord had them do in Tabernacle worship is to temple worship in our dispensation. It all relates to teaching the Father's plan to His children.

Finding Plan of Salvation Symbolism in the Layout of the Tabernacle

The basic layout of the Tabernacle used by the children of Israel was highly symbolic of the three degrees of glory, which are a prominent part of the plan of salvation. The outer courtyard symbolized the telestial kingdom. The first room in the Tabernacle itself, known as the "Holy Place," symbolized the terrestrial kingdom. And the final room in the Tabernacle, "the Holy of Holies" symbolized the celestial kingdom. When the high priest entered through the veil into the Holy of Holies, it was symbolic of entering the presence of the Lord.

The whole layout was symbolic of the various stages of progression His children go through to return to His presence. You can read a summary of the Tabernacle layout in the LDS Bible Dictionary, under "Tabernacle."

As an interesting side note, with perhaps some additional symbolism, the Holy of Holies in the Tabernacle was a perfect cube. According to the Bible Dictionary in our 1979 LDS edition of the Bible, the Tabernacle itself (that stood within the courtyard or Tabernacle grounds) was "30 cubits in length and 10 in breadth and height." This would make it about forty-five feet long, fifteen feet wide, and fifteen feet high. The first of the two compartments within it, the "Holy Place," was thirty feet long and fifteen feet wide. The second compartment, the "Holy of Holies" was fifteen feet by fifteen feet by fifteen feet.

Likewise, the layout of many modern temples includes rooms representing the world (telestial kingdom), the terrestrial kingdom, and the celestial kingdom. (See *Ensign*, January 1972, 54, 63.) In others, especially in smaller temples, this symbolism is incorporated in the presentation of the endowment. The symbolism represents our various stages of progress toward returning to the presence of God in celestial exaltation.

Each temple has a beautiful celestial room, constructed of the finest materials and furnished to remind one of heaven. Faithful members pass through the veil at the end of the endowment session into the celestial room, symbolic of successfully finishing our mortal life and entering back into the presence of God. Our success in so doing is dependent upon our making and keeping covenants that accompany temple worship, finishing our lives as faithful Saints.

Symbolism of Special Clothing Worn by Priests in Ancient Israel

Priests used special clothing as they served in the rites associated with the Tabernacle in ancient Israel. The Lord, in teaching the plan of salvation, uses symbolic clothing. For example, to be clothed in "robes of righteousness" is symbolic of being worthy to be in the presence of God. It symbolizes being clothed in righteous deeds and lifestyles that bring the blessings of celestial glory. It symbolizes being given exaltation.

We find this symbolism in several places in the scriptures. Jacob, Nephi's younger brother, spoke of Judgment Day and the happy state of the righteous who stand before the Savior "clothed" with righteousness.

2 Nephi 9:14 (emphasis added)
14 Wherefore, we shall have a perfect knowledge of all our guilt, and our uncleanness, and our nakedness; and **the righteous** shall have a perfect knowledge of their enjoyment, and their righteousness, **being clothed with purity, yea, even with the robe of righteousness.**

In the Book of Revelation, John saw that righteous martyrs (those who were killed because of living the gospel) were given "white robes." "White robes" symbolize exaltation.

Revelation 6:11 (emphasis added)
11 And **white robes** were given unto every one of them; and it was said unto them, that they should rest yet for a little season, until their fellowservants also and their brethren, that should be killed as they were, should be fulfilled.

In the dedication of the Kirtland Temple, we see this same symbolism of being dressed in robes. In the dedicatory prayer, received as a revelation by the Prophet Joseph Smith, the Prophet spoke of the righteous coming forth in the resurrection to meet the Savior, clothed in clean garments (symbolizing clean lives) and being dressed in "robes of righteousness."

D&C 109:75–76 (emphasis added)
75 That when the trump shall sound for the dead, we shall be caught up in the cloud to meet thee, that we may ever be with the Lord;
76 **That our garments may be pure** [*symbolic of lives made clean through the Atonement of Christ*], that we may be **clothed upon with robes of righteousness** [*symbolic of being given exaltation*], with palms in our hands [*symbolic of triumph and victory*], and crowns of glory upon our heads [*symbolic of exaltation*], and reap eternal joy for all our sufferings.

The doctrine of being made clean and spotless—fit to be in the presence of God—through the Atonement of Christ is clearly taught in the scriptures. "Garments" (meaning "clothing") symbolize our lives. Having our garments made white in the blood of the Lamb is pure Atonement symbolism. It means having our lives made spotless by the Atonement of Jesus Christ. It enables us to be symbolically dressed in robes of righteousness. An example is found in the book of Alma.

Alma 34:36 (emphasis added)
And this I know, because the Lord hath said he dwelleth not in unholy temples, but in the hearts of the righteous doth he dwell; yea, and he has also said that the righteous shall sit down in his kingdom, to go no more out; but **their garments should be made white through the blood of the Lamb.**

The use of special, sacred clothing in conjunction with temple worship today follows the pattern used by the Lord from the beginning to teach the plan of salvation and how to become clean and pure, worthy to be in His presence.

The priests who served in conjunction with the Tabernacle in Old Testament times functioned in the Aaronic Priesthood. Thus, the "high priests" were high priests in the Aaronic Priesthood, not in the Melchizedek Priesthood, as is the case today. We read in the Old Testament that these priests, including Aaron, his sons, and others, who served in the Tabernacle rites and ceremonies wore special sacred clothing, including undergarments. Such ritual clothing can ultimately tie in symbolically with being "clothed in the robe of righteousness" (2 Nephi 9:14) that symbolize being worthy to be in the presence of God.

Knowing that they were commanded by the Lord to wear special clothing can be helpful to modern Latter-day Saints as they take out their own endowments in temples of God. Those who are familiar with the description of the special clothing worn by Aaron and his sons will see our temple robes and clothing as sacred links to the past rather than as something strange.

We can read detailed descriptions of the clothing in Exodus 28 (see following list), and elsewhere. The Lord was very exact in His instructions to Moses for the sacred clothing to be worn by Aaron and his sons as they officiated in rites of the Aaronic Priesthood. This exactness can be symbolic of the exactness required in living the gospel for those who desire exaltation. A scriptural term for "exactness in living the gospel" is the word *just*. In Doctrine and Covenants 76:69, we see the phrase "just men made perfect," describing those who have attained exaltation, who are "priests and kings, who have received of his fulness, and of his glory" (D&C 76:56).

The first item of clothing in the following list was to be worn only by the Aaronic Priesthood high priest. It was made of the finest fabric and was beautiful in design. It was attached to his other ceremonial clothing with gold chains. In biblical color symbolism, gold is symbolic of the best, ultimately symbolic of celestial glory.

- **A breastplate** (verse 4): A breastplate is worn by the high priest only. Served as a Urim and Thummim holder. Also had a different gemstone for each tribe of Israel mounted upon it in four horizontal rows (verses 15–21), symbolizing that Aaron was to keep the tribes of Israel close to his heart as he served them. Representing each of the twelve tribes of Israel with a precious gemstone can symbolize that each of His children is precious to God.

- **An ephod** (verse 4): An *ephod* is an apron (according to the *Old Testament Student Manual,* 152). It is interesting to note that wearing aprons could serve, among other things, as a tie-in to the Garden of Eden when Adam and Eve made aprons after partaking of the fruit of the tree of knowledge of good and evil (Moses 4:13).

- **A robe** (verse 4): Aaron (the high priest) wore a blue robe over the white robe. His sons (the other priests) wore white robes.

- **A mitre, cap, or hat** (verse 4): The high priest's cap had a gold plate attached to the front on which "Holiness to the Lord" was engraved. We see this inscription on our temples today.

- **A girdle or sash** (verse 4): In the *New International Version of the Bible*, the word *sash* is used in place of "girdle" in the King James Bible.

- **"Linen breeches," undergarments, or underpants** (verse 4): "to cover their nakedness" (Exodus 28:42).

Being aware of these articles of special clothing used by priests of the Aaronic Priesthood as they served in the rites of the Tabernacle can be interesting and helpful to temple-goers today.

Before continuing, there are two items of clothing that have symbolic meaning in some cultures—ancient and modern—that have relevance to our temple worship today:

- **Veil over the face**: worn to show reverence and respect before God, and also in the presence of important people (Genesis 24:65).
- **Caps or hats**: worn to show reverence and respect before God. For example, the skullcap or *kippah* worn by many Jewish men and boys symbolizes their awareness of and submission to God. The practice has its roots in biblical times when priests in the Tabernacle and Temple were required to cover their heads.

Temple Clothing Today

Temple clothing is included in the symbolism of temple instruction today. "There is symbolism in the temple ordinances and covenants, their presentation, the physical setting, **and the clothing worn**" (*Ensign*, October 2010, 80; emphasis added).

Several years ago, an article in the *Improvement Era* (replaced by the *Ensign* today) again reminded us that there is symbolism in the sacred clothing worn as part of temple worship. In the article, penned ten years earlier, shortly before his death, Elder John A. Widtsoe of the Quorum of the Twelve taught,

> In the temple all are dressed alike in white. White is the symbol of purity. No unclean person has the right to enter God's house. Besides, the uniform dress symbolizes that before God our Father in Heaven all men

are equal. The beggar and the banker, the learned and the unlearned, the prince and the pauper sit side by side in the temple and are of equal importance if they live righteously before the Lord God. (*Improvement Era*, October 1962, 710)

It is plan of salvation symbolism and it represents, among other things, being clothed in purity and righteousness by accessing the power of the Atonement in our lives. Temple covenants aid us significantly in this process. The clothing symbolizes that we can ultimately stand clean and pure in the presence of God and dwell with Him forever.

This special clothing worn in the temple in association with endowments and sealings was mentioned by President Thomas S. Monson in the priesthood session of the October 2004 general conference. He related the experience of having had the privilege of sealing some dear friends, an older couple, in the temple. Later, the man passed away and President Monson spoke at his funeral. He mentioned seeing the brother in his casket, dressed in his temple clothes.

Shelley died not too long after this period. I had the privilege of speaking at his funeral services. I shall ever see, in memory's eye, the body of my friend Shelley lying in his casket, dressed in his temple clothing. I readily admit the presence of tears, tears of gratitude, for the lost had been found.

Many members today have taken out their own endowments and are familiar with temple clothing. Some who have not yet been to the temple for endowments have attended the viewing of a faithful, endowed member preceding the funeral, as mentioned by President Monson, and have seen the beauty and dignity of the person's temple clothing.

Temple Garments

In the *Endowed from on High* teacher's manual, instruction is given to those preparing to go to the temple for the first time for their endowments. Among other things, they are given guidance on purchasing their own temple garments, including not wearing them before going to the temple.

Those who enter the temple today for their endowments and sealings wear sacred clothing associated with that worship and the covenants entered into there. Sacred underclothing, referred to as "temple garments," is received as a part of the "washings and anointings" in the temple and is worn by faithful members throughout their lives from that point on.

Elder Carlos E. Asay, an emeritus member of the Seventy, spoke of the temple garment as armor.

> There is, however, another piece of armor worthy of our consideration. It is the special underclothing known as the temple garment, or garment of the holy priesthood, worn by members . . . who have received their temple

endowment. This garment, worn day and night, serves three important purposes: it is a reminder of the sacred covenants made with the Lord in His holy house, a protective covering for the body, and a symbol of the modesty of dress and living that should characterize the lives of all the humble followers of Christ. (*Ensign*, August 1997, 18–23)

In the same article, Elder Asay explained,

Latter-day Saints filled with faith wear the garment and wear it properly, not because someone is policing their actions but because they understand the virtues of the sacred clothing and want to "do good and be restored unto that which is good." [*See Alma 41:3.*] On the other hand, when one does not understand the sacred nature of the temple garment, the tendency is to treat it casually and regard it as just another piece of cloth. (Ibid.)

I had an interesting experience many years ago that illustrated the principles associated with the proper wearing of garments taught by Elder Asay. In my early years as a young seminary teacher, I supplemented our income during the summer by working as a welder. On one project, we were working on a steel framework for a partially erected building. One day, another crewmember and I were working about twenty-five to thirty feet off the ground, above a concrete pad on which the building was being built. It was summertime and hot. We were both returned missionaries, and I had noticed that most of the time he did not wear his garments. However, on this day, when our work required that we be high above the concrete, I noticed that he was indeed wearing his garments. I chose not to mention it, but he brought it up. "Dave," he said. "You've probably noticed that I am wearing my garments today. I figured I'd better because it is dangerous up here and I want the protection!" He obviously did not fully understand the sacred nature of temple garments.

In a First Presidency letter to members of the Church, they spoke of the proper wearing of the garment and, among other things, said, "How it is worn is an outward expression of an inward commitment to follow the Savior" (First Presidency Letter, October 10, 1988).

Temple Garments Were Worn by Faithful Saints in Ancient Times

In another quote from the same *Ensign* article by Elder Asay, he explained that faithful Saints in other dispensations have also worn temple garments.

The scriptures contain many references to the wearing of special garments by the ancients. Prior to their expulsion from the Garden of Eden, Adam and Eve were clad in sacred clothing. We read: "Unto Adam also and to his wife did the Lord God make coats of skins, and clothed them" (Genesis 3:21).

They received this clothing in a context of instruction on the Atonement, sacrifice, repentance, and forgiveness (see Moses 5:5–8). The temple garment given to Latter-day Saints is provided in a similar context. It is given to remind wearers of the continuing need for repentance, the need to honor binding covenants made in the house of the Lord, and the need to cherish and share virtue in our daily living so that promised blessings may be claimed. (Ibid.)

Washings and Anointings

President Boyd K. Packer spoke of being washed and anointed in conjunction with modern temple worship: "In the temples, members of the Church who make themselves eligible can participate in the most exalted of the redeeming ordinances that have been revealed to mankind. There, in a sacred ceremony, an individual may be washed and anointed and instructed and endowed and sealed" (*Ensign*, October 2010, 29).

Again, we see similar practices in ancient Tabernacle settings. Aaron and his sons were to be washed, anointed, and consecrated (see heading to Exodus 29 in our LDS edition of the Bible). In verses 1–9 of Exodus, chapter 29, we see:
- Washing with water (verse 4)
- Being dressed in sacred garments and other holy clothing (verses 5–6)
- Being anointed with oil (verse 7)
- Being consecrated (verse 9)

There is much symbolism here. To be "washed" or made ceremonially clean before participating in sacred ordinances symbolizes the power of the Atonement of

Jesus Christ to make us clean from our sins. Symbolically, the waters of baptism wash away our sins and make us worthy to be in the presence of God in His temple now, and then later in His literal presence in celestial glory.

Isaiah instructed his people as follows.

Isaiah 1:16–18

16 Wash you, make you clean; put away the evil of your doings from before mine eyes; cease to do evil;
17 Learn to do well; seek judgment, relieve the oppressed, judge the fatherless, plead for the widow.
18 Come now, and let us reason together, saith the Lord: though your sins be as scarlet, they shall be as white as snow; though they be red like crimson, they shall be as wool.

In Old Testament times, washings and anointings were part of the law of Moses and were used in conjunction with being made clean. They were symbolic of being cleansed by the Atonement of Christ. We see this symbolism in many places. For example,

Leviticus 14:10–20 (emphasis added)

10 And on the eighth day he shall take two he lambs without blemish [*symbolic of the Savior's perfect life*], and one ewe lamb of the first year without blemish, and three tenth deals of fine flour for a meat offering, mingled with oil [*pure olive oil, symbolic of healing, of light from Christ, of the Holy Ghost—D&C 45:55–57, of the Savior's suffering in Gethsemane (the "oil press")*]

under the pressure and weight of our sins], and one log of oil.

11 And the priest that maketh him clean [*symbolic of Christ*] shall present **the man that is to be made clean** [*symbolic of each of us*], and those things, before the Lord, *at* the door of the tabernacle of the congregation:

12 And the priest shall take one he lamb [*symbolic of Christ*], and offer him for a trespass offering [*an atonement*], and the log of oil, and wave them for a wave offering [*see Bible Dictionary, "Feasts" for an explanation of several types of "offerings" associated with ritual feasts*] before the Lord:

13 And he shall slay the lamb in the place where he shall kill the sin offering and the burnt offering, in the holy place: for as the sin offering is the priest's, so is the trespass offering: it is most holy:

14 And **the priest shall take some of the blood** of the trespass offering [*symbolic of the blood of Christ, the Lamb*], and the priest [*similar to and symbolic of ordinance workers in our temples today*] shall put it **upon the tip of the right ear** [*symbolic of hearing and obeying the Lord*] of him that is to be cleansed, and **upon the thumb** [*symbolic of actions, behaviors*] of his right hand [*the covenant hand; symbolic of making covenants with God*], and **upon the great toe of his right foot** [*symbolic of walking in the ways of God*]:

Can you see some additional symbolism in verse 14, above? Christ is spoken of by Paul as "an high priest" in Hebrews 9:11. Thus, symbolically, Christ applies His atoning blood to us and makes us able to hear His voice, act in His work, and walk on His paths.

15 **And the priest shall take some of the** log of **oil, and pour it into the palm of his own left hand:**

16 And the priest shall dip his right finger in the oil that is in his left hand, and shall sprinkle of the oil with his finger seven [*symbolic of becoming perfect through Christ*] times before the Lord:

17 And of the rest of the oil that is in his hand shall the priest put upon **the tip of the right ear** of him that is to be cleansed, and upon **the thumb of his right hand** [*the covenant hand in biblical symbolism; symbolic of making covenants with God*], and upon **the great toe of his right foot,** upon the blood of the trespass offering [*among many possible symbols, one could be that as we take upon us the cleansing blood of Christ through baptism, the Holy Ghost follows up by guiding us to hear, act, and walk in His ways*]:

18 And the remnant of the oil that is in the priest's hand he shall pour **upon the head** of him that is to be cleansed [*symbolic of being anointed in preparation for great blessings from the Lord*]: and the priest shall make an atonement for him before the Lord.

19 And the priest [*symbolizing the Savior*] shall offer the sin offering, and make an **atonement** for him that is to be cleansed from his uncleanness; and afterward he shall kill the burnt offering:

20 And the priest shall offer the burnt offering and the meat offering upon the altar: and the priest shall make an **atonement** for him, **and he shall be clean.**

The oil being used in this Old Testament rite was olive oil. Remember that anointing was also used as preparation for coming blessings and opportunities. For instance, David was anointed to become king (1 Samuel 16:13).

In our day, when Melchizedek Priesthood holders administer to the sick, generally they first anoint the person with consecrated oil in preparation for the coming blessing. This is in accordance with instructions given in James.

James 5:14 (emphasis added)
14 Is any sick among you? let him call for the elders of the church; and let them pray over him, **anointing him with oil** in the name of the Lord:

Christ was "anointed" symbolically in preparation for His Crucifixion and burial by Mary, Martha's sister. The Master responded to the criticism from Judas Iscariot, complaining that the expensive ointment (John 12:3–5) could have been used for better purposes. He said, "For she hath preserved this ointment until now, that she might anoint me in token of my burial" (Joseph Smith Translation, John 12:7).

Name Change and Covenant Making

In ancient times, the changing of one's name was often associated with making covenants with God that would bring increased blessings, as well as additional opportunities and responsibilities. For example, Abraham's name was changed from Abram (Genesis 12:1) to Abraham (Genesis 17:5). His wife's name was changed from Sarai to Sarah (Genesis 17:15).

As stated above, this name change for Abraham was made in conjunction with making covenants with God. The symbolism is that he was, in effect, a new person, a different person than he was before this opportunity to make covenants with God that would lead to exaltation. This symbolism ties in with being "born again" (John 3:5), with a new opportunity for increased progress. It symbolized that he had a broad new set of opportunities and responsibilities in the work of the Lord and that he would someday be a god himself.

Genesis 17:1–7 (emphasis added)
1 And when Abram was ninety years old and nine, the Lord appeared to **Abram**, and said unto him, I am the Almighty God; walk before me, and be thou perfect.
2 And **I will make my covenant between me and thee**, and will multiply thee exceedingly.
3 And Abram fell on his face: and God talked with him, saying,
4 As for me, behold, my covenant is with thee, and **thou shalt be a father of many nations**.
5 **Neither shall thy name any more be called Abram, but thy name shall be Abraham**; for a father of many nations have I made thee.

6 And I will make thee exceeding fruitful, and **I will
make nations of thee, and kings shall come out of
thee** [*this was literally fulfilled for Abraham on this earth,
and also foreshadows the time in which, as a god, he has
infinite posterity*].

7 And **I will establish my covenant between me and
thee** and thy seed after thee in their generations for an
everlasting covenant, to be a God unto thee, and to thy
seed after thee.

Perhaps you've noticed that in patriarchal blessings
today, each recipient of a patriarchal blessing is told one
way or another that he or she is entitled, through personal
worthiness, to the blessings of Abraham, Isaac, and Jacob.
These are the blessings of exaltation (see Abraham 2:9–11).
Temple covenants are covenants required for exaltation.

With the name change for Sarah, the emphasis was on
the greatly increased blessings and responsibilities the Lord
had for her. Again, there is exaltation symbolism here.

Genesis 17:15–16 (emphasis added)
15 And God said unto Abraham, As for Sarai thy wife,
thou shalt not call her name Sarai, but Sarah shall
her name be.

16 And **I will bless her, and give thee a son also of
her**: yea, **I will bless her, and she shall be a mother of
nations; kings of people shall be of her**.

Jacob's name was changed from Jacob to Israel, in
association with promised blessings. His large posterity

became known as the "children of Israel." Again, the name change came in connection with making covenants and resulting blessings. Most of us are evidence of the fulfillment of blessings promised to Jacob. We are descendants of the twelve tribes of Israel (Jacob).

Genesis 32:26–28 (emphasis added)
26 And he said, Let me go, for the day breaketh. And he said, I will not let thee go, except thou **bless me**.
27 And he said unto him, What is thy name? And he said, Jacob.
28 And he said, **Thy name shall be called no more Jacob, but Israel**: for **as a prince hast thou power with God and with men, and hast prevailed**.

Jacob came away from this experience with the angel much more aware of his opportunities and responsibilities in the work of the Lord. The ultimate interpretation of the last two phrases of verse 28, above, "as a prince hast thou power with God and with men, and hast prevailed," is exaltation.

In the Book of Mormon, we read of righteous King Benjamin. Near the beginning of his final address to his people, this great king promised to give his people another name. This new name was to set them apart from all other people.

Mosiah 1:11
11 And moreover, I shall give this people a name, that thereby they may be distinguished above all the people which the Lord God hath brought out of the land of

Jerusalem; and this I do because they have been a diligent people in keeping the commandments of the Lord.

Verse 11, above, in effect becomes the "topic sentence" for Mosiah, chapters 2–5 in which the king teaches his people what it means to be a covenant people of the Lord. Near the end of King Benjamin's address, the people express their willingness to enter into a covenant with the Lord. This led to their being given another name, symbolic of being a new person with greatly increased blessings, opportunities, and responsibilities.

Mosiah 5:5 (emphasis added)

5 And **we are willing to enter into a covenant with our God to do his will, and to be obedient to his commandments in all things that he shall command us, all the remainder of our days,** that we may not bring upon ourselves a never-ending torment, as has been spoken by the angel, that we may not drink out of the cup of the wrath of God.

In the next two verses, King Benjamin summarizes what it will mean for them to be given another name in connection with the covenant they have now made.

Mosiah 5:6–7 (emphasis added)

6 And now, these are the words which king Benjamin desired of them; and therefore he said unto them: Ye have spoken the words that I desired; and **the covenant which ye have made is a righteous covenant.**

7 And now, because of the covenant which ye have made ye shall be called the children of Christ, his sons, and his daughters; for behold, this day he hath spiritually begotten you; for ye say that your hearts are changed through faith on his name; therefore, ye are born of him and have become his sons and his daughters.

Finally, King Benjamin tells the people that the name they will be given is the name of Christ. This symbolizes that they are to be "born again" in Christ, with much increased blessings as they keep the covenant described in verse 5, above. It also symbolizes the freedom that comes with being a true and loyal follower of Christ. And it symbolizes increased accountability and thus opportunity to receive blessings that otherwise would not be available to them.

Mosiah 5:8 (emphasis added)

8 And **under this head ye are made free**, and there is no other head whereby ye can be made free. There is no other name given whereby salvation cometh; therefore, I would that ye should **take upon you the name of Christ**, all you that have entered into the covenant with God that ye should be obedient unto the end of your lives.

A *new name* is mentioned in the book of Revelation, in conjunction with the promise of celestial glory for those who faithfully live the gospel of Jesus Christ.

Revelation 2:17 (emphasis added)

17 He that hath an ear, let him hear what the Spirit saith unto the churches; To him that overcometh will I give to eat of the hidden manna, and will give him a white stone, and in the stone **a new name** written, which no man knoweth saving he that receiveth it.

And in the Doctrine and Covenants, Joseph Smith explained a bit more about the new name mentioned by John in Revelation. It has to do with those who attain celestial glory.

D&C 130:10–11 (emphasis added)

10 Then the white stone mentioned in Revelation 2:17, will become a Urim and Thummim to each individual who receives one, whereby things pertaining to a higher order of kingdoms will be made known;

11 And a white stone is given to each of those who come into the celestial kingdom, whereon is **a new name** written, which no man knoweth save he that receiveth it. The new name is the key word.

In summary, being given another name in the scriptures is symbolic of new blessings and opportunities becoming available by making covenants with God.

Abstaining from Wine and Strong Drink

It is interesting to note that the Lord instructed Aaron and his sons, the Aaronic Priesthood priests who officiated in the Tabernacle, not to drink wine nor strong drink as they served therein. It was symbolic of keeping themselves apart from worldly influences and enabled them to better distinguish between good and evil. The Lord commanded them (pay close attention to verse 10):

Leviticus 10:9–11

9 Do not drink wine nor strong drink, thou, nor thy sons with thee, when ye go into the tabernacle of the congregation, lest ye die: it shall be a statute for ever throughout your generations:

10 And that ye may put difference between holy and unholy, and between unclean and clean;

11 And that ye may teach the children of Israel all the statutes which the Lord hath spoken unto them by the hand of Moses.

Footnote *a* for verse 10, above, in our LDS edition of the Bible explains that in Hebrew, verse 10 can be translated: "To distinguish between the holy and the profane, and between the impure and the pure."

Thus, abstaining from wine and strong drink for these ancient servants of the Lord was symbolic of the ability to distinguish between good and evil and thus keep themselves separate from the ways of the world.

As you are aware, one of the requirements for entrance into our temples today is a current temple recommend. One of the qualifications for it is keeping the Word of Wisdom, which includes abstinence from wine and strong drink. The promises and reasons for keeping the Word of Wisdom are given near the end of Doctrine and Covenants, section 89.

> D&C 89:18–21 (emphasis added)
>
> 18 **And all saints who remember to keep and do these sayings, walking in obedience to the commandments** [*an additional stipulation for receiving these blessings*], **shall receive health in their navel and marrow to their bones** [*a biblical phrase meaning "the support and blessings of the Lord," as was the case with Daniel and his three companions—see Daniel 1:6–20; also see Proverbs 3:7–10*];
>
> 19 **And shall find wisdom and great treasures of knowledge, even hidden treasures** [*meaning, among other things, will have better knowledge and stronger testimonies of the gospel*];
>
> 20 **And shall run and not be weary, and shall walk and not faint** [*they will be strengthened by the Lord and will not be stopped in continuing along the path to exaltation*].

Verse 20, above, should be read in the context of verse 21, next.

> 21 **And I, the Lord, give unto them a promise, that the destroying angel shall pass by them, as the children of Israel, and not slay them**. Amen.

President J. Reuben Clark Jr. explained verse 21 and the three verses preceding it, above, as follows (emphasis added):

This does not say and this does not mean, that to keep the Word of Wisdom is to insure us against death, for death is, in the eternal plan, co-equal with birth. This is the eternal decree. [*1 Corinthians 15:22; 2 Nephi 9:6.*] But it does mean that the destroying angel, he who comes to punish the unrighteous for their sins, as he in olden time afflicted the corrupt Egyptians in their wickedness [*Exodus 12:23, 29*], shall pass by the Saints, "who are walking in obedience to the commandments," and who "remember to keep and do these sayings." **These promises do mean that all those who qualify themselves to enjoy them will be permitted so to live out their lives that they may gain the full experiences and get the full knowledge which they need in order to progress to the highest exaltation in eternity**, all these will live until their work is finished and God calls them back to their eternal home, as a reward. (*Conference Report*, Oct. 1940, 17–18)

Chapter 5: Getting Better at Recognizing Scriptural Symbolism

With this chapter, we will look over several examples of the use of symbolism in the scriptures along with some helps for recognizing and understanding it. The more we become familiar with the use of symbolism used by the Lord and His prophets in the scriptures, the more likely we are to be able to pick up on the symbolism in temple instruction. Seeing the meaning and applying the messages in our lives is the whole point of symbolism.

First, a list of general scriptural symbolism. One symbolic image or concept can take the place of a multitude of words as the Lord and His prophets teach us.

General Scriptural Symbolism

Colors
- **White**: purity; righteousness; exaltation (example: Rev. 3:4–5).
- **Black**: evil; famine; darkness (example: Rev. 6:5–6).
- **Red**: sins; bloodshed (examples: Rev. 6:4; D&C 133:51).

- **Blue**: heaven; godliness; remembering and keeping God's commandments (example: Num. 15:37–40).
- **Green**: life; nature (example: Rev. 8:7).
- **Amber**: sun; light; divine glory (examples: D&C 110:2; Rev. 1:15; Ezek. 1:4, 27; 8:2).
- **Scarlet**: royalty (examples: Dan. 5:29; Matt. 27:28–29).
- **Silver**: worth, but less than gold (examples: Isa. 48:10; 1 Nephi 20:10. The phrase "but not with silver" is deleted in 1 Nephi, perhaps implying that we are not being refined to be second best like silver, rather to be gold, which is the best.)
- **Gold**: the best; exaltation (example: Rev. 4:4).

Body Parts
- **Eye**: perception; light and knowledge.
- **Head**: governing.
- **Ears**: obedience; hearing.
- **Mouth**: speaking.
- **Hair**: modesty; covering.
- **Members**: offices and callings.
- **Heart**: the inner person; courage.
- **Hands**: action, acting.
- **Right hand**: covenant hand; making covenants.
- **Bowels**: center of emotion; whole being.
- **Loins**: posterity; preparing for action (gird up your loins).
- **Liver**: center of feeling.
- **Kidneys**: reins; center of desires, thoughts.
- **Arm**: power.
- **Foot**: mobility; foundation.
- **Toe**: associated with cleansing rites (example: Lev. 14:17).

- **Nose**: anger (examples: 2 Sam. 22:16; Job 4:9).
- **Tongue**: speaking.
- **Blood**: life of the body.
- **Knee**: humility; submission.
- **Shoulder**: strength; effort.
- **Forehead**: total dedication, loyalty (examples: loyalty to God, Rev. 14:1; loyalty to wickedness, Rev. 13:16).

Numbers
- **One**: unity; God.
- **Three**: God, Godhead; a word repeated three times means *superlative*, *most*, or *best* (example: Isa. 6:3).
- **Four**: mankind; earth (see Smith's Bible Dictionary, 1972, 456; example: Rev. 7:1, four angels over four parts of the earth).
- **Seven**: completeness; perfection (example: when man lets God help, it leads to perfection [4 + 3 = 7]).
- **Ten**: numerical perfection (example: Ten Commandments; tithing); well-organized (example: Satan is well-organized, Rev. 13:1).
- **Twelve**: divine government, God's organization (example: Joseph Smith Translation, Rev. 5:6).
- **40 days**: literally 40 days; sometimes means "a long time," as in 1 Sam. 17:16 and—perhaps—Mosiah 7:4.
- **Forever**: endless; can sometimes be a specific period or age, so not endless (see BYU Religious Studies Center Newsletter, Vol. 8, No. 3, May 1994).

Other Symbolism
- **Horse**: victory; power to conquer (examples: Rev. 19:11; Jer. 8:16).

- **Donkey**: peace; submission (example: Christ came in peace at the Triumphal Entry, symbolized by riding on a donkey, Matt. 21:5).
- **Palms**: joy; triumph, victory (examples: John 12:12–13; Rev. 7:9)
- **Wings**: power to move, act (examples: Rev. 4:8; D&C 77:4).
- **Crown**: power; dominion; exaltation (examples: Rev. 2:10; 4:4).
- **Robes**: royalty; kings, queens; exaltation (examples: Rev. 6:11; 7:14; 2 Nephi 9:14; D&C 109:76; 3 Nephi 11:8).

Symbolism in Parables

The Savior used many parables to teach His gospel to the people. Those who understood the symbols generally understood the parables and the messages and instruction in them. Those who did not understand symbolism failed to see the greater lessons.

The idea behind this part of our study of scriptural symbolism is to increase your understanding of symbolism and help get you to the point where you, in effect, automatically look for it and the things that can be taught by it. This can be especially helpful as we attend the temple. With minds tuned to look for the meanings behind symbolism, our temple experiences can be much richer. Included are three of the Master's parables in the New Testament and one from the Doctrine and Covenants. Watch for symbolism. See how much of it you can pick out.

The Parable of the Sower (Matt. 13:3–8)

3 And he spake many things unto them in parables, saying, Behold, a sower went forth to sow;

4 And when he sowed, some seeds fell by the way side, and the fowls came and devoured them up:

5 Some fell upon stony places, where they had not much earth: and forthwith they sprung up, because they had no deepness of earth:

6 And when the sun was up, they were scorched; and because they had no root, they withered away.

7 And some fell among thorns; and the thorns sprung up, and choked them:

8 But other fell into good ground, and brought forth fruit, some an hundredfold, some sixtyfold, some thirtyfold.

Can you pick out the symbolism? The Savior explained how to understand the parable in verses 18–23. We will use bold and add a few bits of commentary, including some from Joseph Smith, as we read these verses.

18 **Hear ye therefore the parable of the sower** [*I will explain the parable of the sower to you*].

19 **When any one heareth the word of the kingdom** [*the gospel*], **and understandeth it not**, then cometh **the wicked one**, and **catcheth away that which was sown in his heart**. This is he which received seed by the way side.

20 But he that received the seed into **stony places**, the same is he that heareth the word, and anon [*immediately*] with joy receiveth it;

21 Yet hath he not root in himself, but dureth [*lasts*] for a while: for when tribulation or persecution ariseth because of the word [*the gospel*], by and by he is offended. 22 He also that received seed **among the thorns** is he that heareth the word [*the gospel*]; and the care of this world, and the deceitfulness of riches, choke the word, and he becometh unfruitful [*does not remain faithful*]. 23 But he that received seed into the **good ground** is he that heareth the word, and understandeth it; [*this takes work and commitment*] which also beareth fruit [*lives the gospel, remains faithful*], and bringeth forth, some an hundredfold, some sixty, some thirty.

JST Matthew 13:21 (verse numbering is sometimes different in the Joseph Smith Translation)

21 But he that received seed into the good ground, is he that heareth the word and understandeth **and endureth**; which also beareth fruit, and bringeth forth, some an hundred-fold, some sixty, and some thirty.

Joseph Smith gave additional insights about the parable of the sower, especially regarding the symbolism in the use of the word *heart* by the Savior.

But listen to the explanation of the parable of the Sower: "When any one heareth the word of the Kingdom, and understandeth it not, then cometh the wicked one, and catcheth away that which was sown in his heart." Now mark the expression—that which was sown in his heart. "This is he which receiveth seed by the way side." [Matthew 13:19.] Men who have no principle of righteousness in themselves, and whose hearts are full of iniquity, and have no desire for the principles of truth, do not understand the word of truth when they hear it. The devil taketh away the word of truth out of their hearts, because there is no desire for righteousness in them. "But he that receiveth seed in stony places, the same is he that heareth the word, and anon, with joy receiveth it; yet hath he not root in himself, but dureth for a while: for when tribulation or persecution ariseth because of the word, by and by, he is offended. He also that receiveth seed among the thorns, is he that heareth the word; and the care of this world, and the deceitfulness of riches choke the word, and he becometh unfruitful. But he that received seed into the good ground is he that heareth the word, and understandeth it, which also beareth fruit, and bringeth forth, some an hundred fold, some sixty, some thirty." Thus the Savior Himself explains unto His disciples the parable which He put forth, and left no mystery or darkness upon the minds of those who firmly believe on His words.

We draw the conclusion, then, that the very reason why the multitude, or the world, as they were designated by the Savior, did not receive an explanation upon His parables, was because of unbelief. To you, He says, (speaking to His disciples,) it is given to know the mysteries of the Kingdom of God. And why?

Because of the faith and confidence they had in Him. (*Teachings of the Prophet Joseph Smith*, 1976, 97)

The Parable of the Wheat and the Tares (Matt. 13:24–30)
24 Another parable put he forth unto them, saying, The kingdom of heaven is likened unto a man which sowed good seed in his field:

25 But while men slept, his enemy came and sowed tares among the wheat, and went his way.

26 But when the blade was sprung up, and brought forth fruit, then appeared the tares also.

27 So the servants of the householder came and said unto him, Sir, didst not thou sow good seed in thy field? from whence then hath it tares?

28 He said unto them, An enemy hath done this. The servants said unto him, Wilt thou then that we go and gather them up?

29 But he said, Nay; lest while ye gather up the tares, ye root up also the wheat with them.

30 Let both grow together until the harvest: and in the time of harvest I will say to the reapers, Gather ye together first the tares, and bind them in bundles to burn them: but gather the wheat into my barn.

Again, can you pick out the symbolism? It takes practice. Here, again, the Savior gave the explanation of the parable. It is found in verses 36–43. We will include in these verses some notes, emphasis with bold, and commentary along with helps from the Joseph Smith Translation.

36 Then Jesus sent the multitude away, and went into the house: and his disciples came unto him, saying, Declare [*explain*] unto us the parable of the tares of the field [*verses 24–30*].

37 He answered and said unto them, **He that soweth** [*plants*] the good seed [*wheat; righteousness*] **is the Son of man** [*Christ; Son of Man of Holiness—see Moses 6:57*];

38 **The field is the world**; the **good seed are the children of the kingdom** [*faithful members of the Church; the righteous*]; but the **tares are the children of the wicked one** [*followers of Satan; the wicked*];

39 The **enemy that sowed them is the devil**; the **harvest is the end of the world**; and the **reapers** [*harvesters*] **are the angels.**

40 As therefore the tares [*the wicked*] are gathered and burned in the fire; so shall it be in the end of this world [*the wicked will be burned at the Second Coming*].

41 The Son of man [*Christ*] shall send forth his angels, and they shall gather out of his kingdom all things that offend, and them which do iniquity [*the wicked*];

42 And shall cast them into a furnace of fire [*the burning at the Second Coming—see note above*]: there shall be wailing [*bitter crying*] and gnashing [*grinding*] of teeth.

43 Then shall the righteous shine forth as the sun [*symbolic of celestial glory for the righteous saints*] in the kingdom of their Father. Who hath ears to hear, let him hear [*those who are spiritually in tune will understand what I am saying*].

Joseph Smith Translation, Matthew 13:39–44

39 The harvest is the end of the world, or the destruction of the wicked.

40 The reapers are the angels, or the messengers sent of heaven.

41 As, therefore, the tares are gathered and burned in the fire, so shall it be in the end of this world, or the destruction of the wicked.

42 For in that day, before the Son of man shall come, he shall send forth his angels and messengers of heaven.

43 And they shall gather out of his kingdom all things that offend, and them which do iniquity, and shall cast them out among the wicked; and there shall be wailing and gnashing of teeth.

44 For the world shall be burned with fire.

The Parable of the Leaven (Matt. 13:33)

33 Another parable spake he unto them; The kingdom of heaven is like unto leaven, which a woman took, and hid in three measures of meal, till the whole was leavened.

This is a short one. You'll need to know that *leaven* functions like yeast in making bread dough rise. Joseph Smith explained the symbolism in this parable. He said that the "leaven" in verse 33 could be compared to the true Church as it expands into the whole world (*Teachings of the Prophet Joseph Smith*, 100, 102).

A Parable from the Doctrine and Covenants

The Savior used a parable in the Doctrine and Covenants, section 101, to explain why members of the Church who had settled in Missouri in anticipation of establishing Zion had been driven out. This parable is a good study for us in picking out symbolism and its meanings. It is also helpful in showing us how to see the "side messages" to the symbolism, or in other words the applications to our own lives based on the symbolism in the parable.

First, some background. Beginning in July of 1833, mobs began attacking the Saints in Jackson County, Missouri, destroying their homes and driving them from the county. For example, on the night of Thursday, October 31, 1833, "a mob of about fifty horsemen attacked the Whitmer settlement on the Big Blue River, west of Independence. They unroofed thirteen houses and nearly whipped to death several men, including Hiram Page, one of the eight witnesses of the Book of Mormon" (*Church History in the Fulness of Times*, 1989, 135–136).

By the time of this revelation, most Church members in Jackson County had fled across the Missouri River into Clay County, where local citizens helped them by offering shelter, food, clothing, and work as much as their own circumstances permitted. Members lived in abandoned slave cabins, built crude shacks, and lived in tents throughout the rest of the winter. Members of the mobs in Jackson County called the citizens of Clay County "Jack-Mormons" because they were friendly toward the Saints.

Needless to say, being driven from their lands and property was a great disappointment to the Saints. They had anticipated that Zion would be built up at this time in Missouri and looked forward to being a part of it.

The Parable Concerning the Redemption of Zion
Doctrine & Covenants 101:43–62 (emphasis added)
43 And now, **I will show unto you a parable**, that you may know my will **concerning the redemption of Zion**.
44 A certain **nobleman** [*Christ—see verse 52*] had a **spot of land** [*Zion, in Jackson County, Missouri*], very choice; and he said unto **his servants** [*members of the Church who were called to go to Zion*]: Go ye unto **my vineyard** [*Jackson County*], even upon **this very choice piece of land** [*Zion*], and **plant twelve olive trees** [*establish LDS settlements*];

Twelve in scriptural symbolism means God's divine organization and work. Thus, twelve in verse 44, above, would not mean literally twelve settlements, but rather communities that represent God and His work of restoring the gospel in the latter days.

45 And set **watchmen** [*prophets; Church leaders*] round about them, and build a **tower** [*temple*], that **one** [*the local leaders of the Church*] **may overlook the land round about** [*may see and spot approaching danger, especially spiritual dangers*], **to be a watchman upon the tower** [*to guard against the evils and dangers of the world*], that mine **olive trees** [*the members and their new*

settlements] may not be broken down when the enemy shall [*not* if *but* when *dangers come*] come to spoil and take upon themselves the fruit of my vineyard.

46 Now, **the servants of the nobleman** [*the Saints who went to Missouri*] went and did as their lord commanded them [*moved to the land of Zion*], and planted the olive trees [*established LDS settlements*], and **built a hedge** round about [*established their territory*], and **set watchmen** [*local leaders of the Church*], and **began to build a tower** [*began to build a temple*].

Remember that the Lord had already designated the site for this temple (see D&C 57:3), and the Prophet Joseph Smith had already dedicated it (D&C 84:3). Watch now as the parable continues, how the members in Zion rationalized away the importance of the temple and began making their own rules and priorities rather than obeying the Lord's commandments.

47 And **while they were yet laying the foundation thereof** [*of the temple, as they did lay the cornerstones of the temple*], **they began to say among themselves**: And **what need hath my lord of this tower?**

48 And **consulted for a long time** [*began procrastinating*], saying among themselves: **What need hath my lord of this tower, seeing this is a time of peace?** [*See verse 8.*]

49 **Might not this money be given to the exchangers?** [*Couldn't we make better use of this money?*] For **there is no need of these things**.

Remember, the Lord said, in verse 41, that some were faithful, but others were not. This obviously led to disharmony, to "jarrings and contentions" (verse 6), which are not compatible with the celestial laws and principles that Zion was to be established upon (D&C 105:5).

As we see, beginning with the following verse 50, such lack of harmony and unity with respect to commitments and covenants each of them had already made opened the door to mob violence against them, ending with the failure to establish Zion at that time.

50 And **while they were at variance one with another** they became very slothful, and they hearkened not unto the commandments of their lord.

51 And **the enemy came by night** [*symbolizing that they did not expect trouble*], and **broke down the hedge** [*broke through the inadequate defenses of the Saints, spiritually as well as physically*]; and **the servants of the nobleman** [*the members of the Church in* Zion] **arose and were affrighted, and fled**; and **the enemy** [*the mobs; symbolic of Satan*] **destroyed their works**, and **broke down the olive trees** [*destroyed the LDS settlements in Zion*].

Afterward, the Lord chastens these members for failing to obey His commandments and establish Zion.

52 Now, behold, the nobleman, the lord of the vineyard, called upon his servants, and said unto them, **Why! what is the cause of this great evil?**

53 **Ought ye not to have done even as I commanded you, and**—after ye had planted the vineyard, and built the hedge round about, and set watchmen upon the walls thereof—**built the tower also**, and set a watchman upon the tower, and watched for my vineyard, **and not have fallen asleep, lest the enemy should come upon you?**

Verse 54, next, gives us strong reason to carefully study and heed the words of our living prophets:

54 And behold, **the watchman upon the tower would have seen the enemy while he was yet afar off**; and then **ye could have made ready** and kept the enemy from breaking down the hedge thereof, and saved my vineyard from the hands of the destroyer.

Beginning with verse 55, Joseph Smith is instructed to gather a small army from the membership in the Kirtland area and elsewhere, which will become known as "Zion's Camp." They are to march to Missouri and help the Saints there.

55 And **the lord of the vineyard** [*Christ*] said unto **one of his servants** [*Joseph Smith—see D&C 103:21*]: Go and **gather** together the residue of my servants, and take all the strength of mine house, which are **my warriors**, my young men, and they that are of middle age also among all my servants, who are the strength of mine house, save [*except*] those only whom I have

appointed to tarry [*those who are to remain behind to lead the Church while Joseph and the others march the 900 miles to Missouri*];

56 And **go ye** straightway [*right away*] **unto the land of my vineyard** [*Jackson County, Missouri*], and **redeem my vineyard**; for it is mine; **I have bought it with money** [*the Saints in Zion had paid for their properties and had legal title to the lands from which they were driven*].

As you can see, verse 57, next, contains terms and symbolism of warfare in ancient times.

57 **Therefore, get ye straightway unto my land; break down the walls of mine enemies; throw down their tower, and scatter their watchmen.**

Notice that there is a significant lesson in the timing of the Lord in these verses? We see the phrase "by and by" in verse 58, next. And in verses 59 and 60, we see the servant asking, in effect, when Zion will be redeemed. And the Lord answers, "When I will." One of the lessons we must learn is that when the Lord commands, we must obey now. In some cases, people basically say that they will obey after they see the blessings and make sure that the effort to obey is worthwhile. However, that is not how it works.

In this case, the Saints are told what to do "straightway" (verses 56, 57, 60, 62), but the desired results will take place "when I will" (verse 60), in other words, in the Lord's due time.

58 And inasmuch as they gather together against you, avenge me of mine enemies, **that by and by** [*eventually; in the Lord's due time*] **I may come with the residue** [*perhaps meaning the righteous remnant of Israel—compare with 3 Nephi 5:24; Ether 13:10*] **of mine house and possess the land.**

59 And the servant said unto his lord: **When shall these things be?**

60 And he said unto his servant: **When I will**; go ye straightway, and **do all things whatsoever I have commanded you;**

In verse 61, the Savior compliments and gives approval to Joseph Smith. At the end of verse 62, we see that it was to be a long time before Zion would be established in Missouri.

61 And **this shall be my seal** [*the Lord's approval and covenant*] **and blessing upon you** [*Joseph Smith, see verse 55*]—a faithful and wise steward in the midst of mine house, a ruler in my kingdom.

62 And **his servant went straightway, and did all things whatsoever his lord commanded him**; and **after many days all things were fulfilled**.

In the *Doctrine and Covenants Student Manual,* 1981 edition, page 243, a quote by Sidney B. Sperry is given, in which he explains the above parable as follows:

It would seem that the parable is to be interpreted in this way: the nobleman is the Lord, whose choice land in His vineyard is Zion in Missouri. The places where the Saints live in Zion are the olive trees. The servants are the Latter-day Saint settlers, and the watchmen are their officers in the Church. While yet building in Zion, they become at variance with each other and do not build the tower or Temple whose site had been dedicated as early as August 3, 1831. Had they built it as directed, it would have been a spiritual refuge for them, for from it the Lord's watchmen could have seen by revelation the movements of the enemy from afar. This foreknowledge would have saved them and their hard work when the enemy made his assault.

But the Saints in Missouri were slothful, lax, and asleep. The enemy came, and the Missouri persecutions were the result. The Lord's people were scattered and much of their labors wasted. The Almighty rebuked His people, as we have already seen, but He commanded one of His servants (55), Joseph Smith (103:21), to gather the "strength of Mine house" and rescue His lands and possessions gathered against them.

Subsequently, the Prophet and his brethren in the famous Zion's Camp did go to Missouri in 1834 in an attempt to carry out the terms of the parable. Before they went, additional revelation was received (see 103:21–28) concerning the redemption of Zion. The brethren were instructed to try to buy land in Missouri, not to use force; and if the enemy came against them, they were to bring a curse upon them. Zion was not redeemed at that time but we may look for it in the not-too-distant future. Verily, it will be redeemed when the Lord wills it (Compendium, 521–522).

Though Joseph Smith followed the Lord's instructions to gather together the "strength of my house" (D&C 103:22) by organizing Zion's Camp to redeem Zion, the Lord's purpose in sending them and his will concerning the redemption of Zion were not fully understood by his people. The redemption of Zion did not take place at that time. When the servant in the parable asked when the land would be possessed, the Lord responded, "When I will" (D&C 101:60).

The parable further states that all things will be fulfilled "after many days" (vs. 62), which passage indicates that a long period of time will pass before Zion will be redeemed. The redemption of Zion still had not taken place even after the Saints had been expelled from Missouri and from Nauvoo. The Lord then told Brigham Young that "Zion shall be redeemed in mine own due time" (D&C 136:18). The redemption of Zion (meaning, the city of New Jerusalem in Missouri) is still future, although of course it is much closer now than it was when the Saints first sought to regain their inheritance in the land of Zion.

The time of Zion's redemption is referred to in Doctrine and Covenants 58:44; 105:15, 37. Compare the parable in Doctrine and Covenants 101 with those given in Isaiah 5:1–7 and Matthew 21:33–46.

Other Examples of Scriptural Symbolism

Symbolism of Baptism by Immersion

The Apostle Paul used symbolism to teach the significance of baptism by immersion. Pay close attention to his careful use of highly descriptive words as he teaches us that when we are baptized, we effectively bury our old sinful selves with Christ in the grave. Then, we come forth with Christ as new people, "born again," starting a new life of dedication to the gospel and personal righteousness. It is a fresh start. We have been symbolically washed clean of past sins and the corrupt elements of our old lives.

Romans 6:3–6

3 Know ye not, that so many of us as were baptized into Jesus Christ were baptized into his death?

4 Therefore we are buried with him by baptism into death [*being buried in the waters of baptism is symbolic of accepting Christ's invitation to join Him in burying our sinful selves and thus letting our sinful ways die*]: that like as Christ was raised up from the dead by the glory of the Father, even so we also should walk in newness of life [*so that, just as Christ came forth from the grave in glory, we can come forth from the waters of baptism into a new life filled with the glory and influence of the Father*].

5 For if we have been planted [*buried*] together in the likeness of his death [*if we have buried our old sinful lives, through His Atonement*], we shall be also in the

likeness of his resurrection [*we will have a glorious new life in the gospel*]:

In verse 6, next, Paul uses a very strong word to describe the effort sometimes needed on our part to repent of sins. He uses the word *crucify*. This is really strong symbolism! It implies that some sins require great pain and godly sorrow to be rid of them. Indeed, changing friends, being cut off from family, going through withdrawals from chemical dependency, confessing serious sin to the bishop and facing possible consequences, refraining from Sabbath-breaking activities, cutting back on expenses in order to pay an honest tithe, and so forth can be painful, but walking in "newness of life" (verse 4) makes it more than worthwhile to "crucify" our sins.

6 Knowing this, that our old man [*our old lifestyle*] is crucified with him [*Christ*], that the body of sin [*our past sins*] might be destroyed, that henceforth [*from now on*] we should not serve sin.

There is additional symbolism here. As you get more familiar with symbolism, you will want to look for secondary symbolism beyond the obvious. There is possibly some in the above verses about baptism symbolism. One possibility is that the Savior described Himself as "living water" (John 4:10). Thus, some secondary symbolism here could be that as we immerse ourselves in the "living waters" (Jer. 2:13) of Christ, our lives become new, fresh, and clean. We are constantly renewed and refreshed by the gospel of Jesus Christ.

Symbolism in Animal Sacrifices

After Adam and Eve were cast out of the Garden of Eden, which was a vital part of the Father's plan, Adam was commanded to build an altar and offer animal sacrifices (*Doctrines of Salvation*, Vol. 2, 232). In Moses 5:4–7, Adam and Eve were taught that the animal sacrifices Adam was commanded to offer, in obedience to the commandment of the Lord, were symbolic of the Savior's sacrifice for all mankind. Let's read through these verses and see what symbolism becomes clear to us.

Moses 5:4–7

4 And Adam and Eve, his wife, called upon the name of the Lord, and they heard the voice of the Lord from the way toward the Garden of Eden, speaking unto them, and they saw him not; for they were shut out from his presence.

5 And he gave unto them commandments, that they should worship the Lord their God, and should offer the firstlings of their flocks, for an offering unto the Lord. And Adam was obedient unto the commandments of the Lord.

6 And after many days an angel of the Lord appeared unto Adam, saying: Why dost thou offer sacrifices unto the Lord? And Adam said unto him: I know not, save the Lord commanded me.

7 And then the angel spake, saying: This thing is a similitude of the sacrifice of the Only Begotten of the Father, which is full of grace and truth.

Were you able to pick out some symbolism? Here are a few possibilities:

- In verse 5, "firstlings" means "the firstborn." Thus, the symbolism is that the "Firstborn" of the Father's spirit children—in other words, Jesus Christ—would be sacrificed for our sins.

- Did you notice that verse 5 says "their flocks"? The sacrificial animal has to come from their own herd, not someone else's. It has to be a personal and voluntary sacrifice on the part of the person offering the sacrifice. The symbolism is that the Savior's sacrifice would be utterly personal and voluntary.

- The altar upon which the sacrifices were offered would be symbolic of the "altar cross" upon which Christ would give His life.

- In verse 7, Adam and Eve are taught the direct symbolism of the sacrifices: "This thing is a similitude of the sacrifice of the Only Begotten of the Father." In other words, the angel instructs them that the sacrifices Adam has been offering are symbolic of the Savior's sacrifice.

- The symbolism in the last phrase of verse 7, "which is full of grace and truth," includes the fact that the Savior is fully capable of saving us (in the simplest definition, "grace" means "help") and can supply us with pure truth to base our lives on, such that we can fully access His grace.

Secondary Symbolism

To better understand symbolism, a desirable skill to develop is recognizing what might be termed "secondary" symbolism. Some examples can be pointed out in connection with Moses 5:4–7, above.

- Adam and Eve had become mortal and were doing their part to keep the commandments of God, as given them at that point. An angel appeared and taught them about the Atonement symbolism involved in sacrificing the firstlings of their flocks. Secondary symbolism would include the fact that God is always aware of His children on earth and has a pattern of sending messengers, both heavenly and mortal, to teach and bless them.

- Another piece of secondary symbolism could be that Adam and Eve are taught, as are we, that willingness to sacrifice our all as needed for the growth and spread of the gospel is necessary for us to successfully grow in the gospel and ultimately return to the presence of the Father.

- Another aspect of secondary symbolism from this set of verses might be the importance of faith and obedience in our lives. Adam did not know why he was offering sacrifices, only that he had been commanded to do so. The symbolism of his act of obedience transfers to us. We do not always understand the reasons for the commandments of God, yet we are to faithfully keep them. When we do so, it opens the door for additional revelation and knowledge.

- Another point of secondary symbolism could be that, just as Adam offered the best that he had to offer on the altar, we too offer our best to God on the altar of sacrifice. "Sacrifice brings forth the blessings of heaven"

(*Hymns*, 1985, "Praise to the Man," 27). Activity in the Church brings with it all kinds of opportunities to sacrifice our best by way of service, time, talents, money, effort, kindness, and so forth.

- Altars are associated with worshipping God. We kneel at the altar of the temple when we are sealed for time and eternity to our eternal companion. We symbolically commit our best to each other and to the Lord upon the altar.

- Yet another facet of secondary symbolism from these verses could be that we have tangible, physical contact and association with God by proxy through His servants and messengers, including angels, prophets, bishops, and stake presidents.

Doctrine & Covenants 1:38 (emphasis added)
38 What I the Lord have spoken, I have spoken, and I excuse not myself; and though the heavens and the earth pass away, my word shall not pass away, but shall all be fulfilled, **whether by mine own voice or by the voice of my servants, it is the same**.

More Symbolism from the Scriptures

The Atonement of Jesus Christ is the central focus of the plan of salvation. It enables each of the Father's children to return, ultimately, clean and pure to His presence if he or she makes wise choices when properly taught and given a fair chance. Much symbolism is used throughout the scriptures to teach this vital element of the "great plan of happiness" (Alma 42:8).

We will go to the book of Leviticus in the Old Testament and look at an example of such that is often missed by members of the Church. We will first look at the scripture block without notes. Afterward, we will study the same verses with notes and commentary. As you read the passages without notes, see if you can spot some Atonement symbolism. Then see if the explanatory notes provide any new insights for you as to how the Lord uses symbolism to teach His plan to us.

First, the verses without commentary.

Leviticus 14:1–9

1 And the Lord spake unto Moses, saying,

2 This shall be the law of the leper in the day of his cleansing: He shall be brought unto the priest:

3 And the priest shall go forth out of the camp; and the priest shall look, and, behold, if the plague of leprosy be healed in the leper;

4 Then shall the priest command to take for him that is to be cleansed two birds alive and clean, and cedar wood, and scarlet, and hyssop:

5 And the priest shall command that one of the birds be killed in an earthen vessel over running water:

6 As for the living bird, he shall take it, and the cedar wood, and the scarlet, and the hyssop, and shall dip them and the living bird in the blood of the bird that was killed over the running water:

7 And he shall sprinkle upon him that is to be cleansed from the leprosy seven times, and shall pronounce him clean, and shall let the living bird loose into the open field.

8 And he that is to be cleansed shall wash his clothes, and shave off all his hair, and wash himself in water, that he may be clean: and after that he shall come into the camp, and shall tarry abroad out of his tent seven days.

9 But it shall be on the seventh day, that he shall shave all his hair off his head and his beard and his eyebrows, even all his hair he shall shave off: and he shall wash his clothes, also he shall wash his flesh in water, and he shall be clean.

Now, the verses with notes and commentary. First, some brief background:

The above verses of Leviticus, chapter 14, deal with the ritual cleansing of lepers. Leprosy itself was a contagious, much-dreaded and feared disease of the skin, considered to be a "living death" (see Bible Dictionary, "Leper"). It led to nerve paralysis and deformation of the body's extremities. Under the law of Moses, lepers were prohibited from direct physical contact with others (because of their fear of spreading the disease) and were required to live outside the camp of the children of Israel during their years in the wilderness. Later, after Israel had entered the promised land, lepers were forbidden to enter walled cities.

The cleansing of the ten lepers in Luke 17:12–19 who were standing "afar off" from Christ is not only an example of the Savior's power over physical disease, but represents His miraculous power to heal us spiritually, through our faith in Him (Luke 17:19). We see His power to cleanse and heal us symbolized in these verses of Leviticus. Keep in mind that there are many different ways to view and interpret symbols. What is presented here is one approach at interpreting this symbolism.

Leviticus 14:1–9 (emphasis added)
1 And the Lord spake unto Moses, saying,
2 This shall be **the law of the leper** [*the rules for being made clean; symbolic of serious sin and great need for help and cleansing*] **in the day of his cleansing** [*symbolic of the opportunity to be made spiritually clean and pure*]:
He shall be brought unto the priest [*authorized servant of God; bishop, stake president, one who holds the keys of authority to act for God*]:
3 And **the priest shall go forth out of the camp** [*the person with leprosy did not have fellowship with the Lord's people and was required to live outside the main camp of the children of Israel; the bishop, symbolically, goes out of the way to help sinners who want to repent*];
and **the priest shall look, and, behold, if the plague of leprosy be healed in the leper** [*the bishop serves as a judge in Israel to see if the repentant sinner is ready to return to full membership privileges*];
4 Then shall the priest command to take for him that is to be cleansed [*the person who has repented*] **two birds** [*one represents the Savior during His mortal mission, the other represents the person who has repented*] alive and clean, and **cedar wood** [*symbolic of the cross*], and

scarlet [*associated with mocking Christ before the Crucifixion, Mark 15:17*], and **hyssop** [*associated with Christ on the cross, John 19:29*]:

5 And the priest shall command that **one of the birds** [*symbolic of the Savior*] be **killed in an earthen vessel** [*symbolic of the earth, to which Christ was sent to die for us*] **over running water** [*Christ offers living water, the gospel of Jesus Christ—John 7:37–38, which cleanses us when we come unto Him*]:

6 As for the living bird [*representing the person who has repented*], **he** [*the priest; symbolic of the bishop, stake president, one who holds the keys of judging in God's kingdom*] **shall take it** [*the living bird*], **and the cedar wood**, and the **scarlet**, and the **hyssop** [*all associated with the Atonement of Christ*], **and shall dip them and the living bird in the blood of the bird that was killed over the running water** [*representing the cleansing power of the Savior's blood which was shed for us*]:

7 And he shall **sprinkle upon him that is to be cleansed from the leprosy** [*symbolically, being cleansed from sin*] **seven times** [*seven is the number that, in biblical numeric symbolism, represents completeness, perfection, God's work*], **and shall pronounce him clean** [*he has been forgiven*], **and shall let the living bird** [*the person who has repented*] **loose into the open field** [*representing the wide open opportunities again available in the kingdom of God for the person who truly repents*].

8 And **he that is to be cleansed shall wash his clothes** [*symbolic of cleaning up your life from sinful ways and pursuits—compare with Isaiah 1:16*], and **shave off all his hair** [*symbolic of becoming like a newborn baby; fresh start, "born again"*], and **wash himself in water** [*symbolic of baptism*], **that he may be clean** [*cleansed from sin*]: and **after that he shall come into the camp** [*rejoin the Lord's covenant people*], and shall tarry abroad out of his tent seven days.

9 But it shall be on the seventh day, that he shall shave all his hair off his head and his beard and his eyebrows, even all his hair he shall shave off [*symbolic of being "born again"*]: and he shall wash his clothes [*clean up his life—garments or clothing was symbolic of one's life*], also he shall wash his flesh in water [*symbolic of baptism*], and he shall be clean [*a simple fact, namely that we can repent and truly be cleansed and healed by the Savior's Atonement*].

Understanding Symbolism in Isaiah's Writings

Many people have considerable difficulty understanding the writings of Isaiah because of the symbolism he uses. This is an area where most of us need help. However, once we get a feel for his symbolic writing, we can learn much by studying his writings. The following examples can be helpful in increasing our ability to understand and benefit from symbolism used in the scriptures. This skill can transfer, with the help of the Spirit, to our understanding of the temple endowment.

Isaiah 1:1–18 (emphasis added)

1 **The vision of Isaiah** the son of Amoz, which he saw **concerning Judah and Jerusalem** in the days of Uzziah, Jotham, Ahaz, and Hezekiah, kings of Judah [*the kings mentioned above reigned from about 740 to 701 BC*].

Isaiah states the main problem in verses 2–4, next.

2 Hear, O heavens, and give ear, O earth: for the Lord hath spoken, **I have nourished and brought up children, and they have rebelled against me.**

3 The ox knoweth his owner, and the ass his master's crib [*manger*]: but **Israel doth not know** [*know God*], my people doth not consider [*think seriously; that is to say, Israel, animals are wiser than you are!*].

4 Ah **sinful nation**, a **people laden with iniquity** [*loaded down with wickedness*], a seed of evildoers, children that are **corrupters**: they **have forsaken the Lord**, they have provoked the Holy One of Israel unto anger, they **are gone away backward** [*retrogressing; they have chosen to be "in the world" and "of the world"*].

5 **Why should ye be stricken any more** [*why do you keep asking for more punishment*]? ye will revolt more and more: **the whole head** [*leadership*] **is sick**, and the whole heart [*the people*] faint [*is diseased; in other words, are spiritually sick*].

Isaiah continues the theme that the whole nation is riddled with wickedness and spiritual sickness. He uses repetition to drive home the point.

6 **From the sole of the foot even unto the head there is no soundness in it** [*you are completely sick*]; but **wounds, and bruises, and putrifying** [*filled with pus*] **sores** [*symbolically saying that the people are spiritually beaten and infected with sin*]: **they have not been closed, neither bound up, neither mollified with ointment** [*you are sick and you don't even care; you won't try the simplest first aid: the Atonement of Christ*].

Old Testament prophets often spoke prophetically of the future as if it had already happened. Isaiah uses this technique as he prophesies of the impending captivity of these wicked people.

7 **Your country is desolate**, your cities are **burned** with fire: your land, strangers [*foreigners*] devour it in your presence, and it is desolate, as overthrown by strangers [*foreigners, specifically the Assyrians*].

8 And **the daughter of Zion** [*Israel*] **is left as a cottage** [*temporary shade structure built of straw and leaves*] in a vineyard, as a lodge [*same as cottage*] in a garden of cucumbers, as a besieged city [*you are about as secure as a flimsy shade shack in a garden*].

9 **Except the Lord of hosts had left unto us a very small remnant** [*if God hadn't intervened and saved a few of Israel*], **we should have been as Sodom**, and we should have been like unto Gomorrah [*completely destroyed*].

10 **Hear the word of the Lord, ye rulers of Sodom** [*"Listen up, you wicked leaders!"*]; **give ear unto the**

law of our God, ye people of Gomorrah [*Sodom and Gomorrah symbolize total wickedness*].

11 **To what purpose is the multitude of your sacrifices unto me** [*what good are your insincere, empty rituals*]? saith the Lord: I am full ["I've had it up to here!"] of the burnt offerings of rams, and the fat of fed beasts; and I delight not in the blood of bullocks, or of lambs, or of he goats.

12 When ye come to appear before me, who **hath required this at your hand, to tread my courts** [*who authorized you hypocrites to act religious and worship me*]?

13 **Bring no more vain** [*useless*] **oblations** [*offerings*]; incense is an abomination unto me; the new moons [*special Sabbath ritual at beginning of month—see Bible Dictionary, "New Moon"*] and sabbaths, the calling of assemblies, I cannot ["*I can't stand it!*"] away with; it is iniquity, even the solemn meeting [*solemn assembly*].

14 **Your new moons and your appointed feasts** [*your hypocritical worship*] **my soul hateth**: they are a trouble unto me; I am weary to bear them.

15 And **when ye spread forth your hands** [*when you pray*], **I will hide mine eyes from you**: yea, when ye make many prayers, **I will not hear**: your hands are full of blood [*bloodshed; murder—see verse 21*].

Next, in spite of the gross wickedness of these people, as described by Isaiah, they are invited by a merciful Savior to repent and return to Him. Major message: if you want to repent but you think your sins have put you beyond the reach of the Savior's Atonement, think again.

16 **Wash you** [*be baptized*], make you clean; put away the evil of your doings from before mine eyes [*repent*]; cease to do evil;

17 **Learn to do well** [*don't just cease to do evil, but replace evil with good*]; seek judgment [*be fair*], relieve the oppressed, judge the fatherless [*be kind and fair to them*], plead for [*stand up for, defend*] the widow.

Verse 18, next, is among the best known of all Isaiah's quotes. With verses 1–15 as a backdrop, this verse wonderfully and clearly teaches the power of the Atonement of Jesus Christ to cleanse and heal completely.

18 Come now, and let us reason together, saith the Lord: **though your sins be as scarlet** [*cloth dyed with scarlet, a color-fast dye*], **they shall be as white as snow** [*even though you think your sins are "colorfast," the Atonement can cleanse you*]; **though they be red like crimson, they shall be as wool** [*a long process is required to get wool white, but it can be done*].

Another chapter of Isaiah that is rich in symbolism—including Atonement symbolism—is chapter 6, in which he receives the call to serve as a prophet. He feels inadequate and expresses it in common expressions and symbolism of his day (verse 5). His concerns about his unworthiness and inadequacies are addressed wonderfully by the Atonement of Christ, as seen in the beautiful Atonement symbolism contained in verses 6 and 7. With the confidence that comes through being made clean by the Savior's atoning sacrifice, he accepts the call (verse 8) and goes forth to serve. Watch how an understanding of symbolism brings the scriptures to life.

Background

Chapter 6 contains some rich Atonement symbolism, especially verses 6 and 7. Without an understanding of symbolism, these two verses seem strange and mysterious. With it, they show the wonderful power of the Atonement of Christ to heal and enable us to accept difficult callings with assurance and faith.

Most scholars agree that this chapter is an account of Isaiah's call to serve as a prophet of the Lord. Some feel that it is a later calling to a major assignment. Either way, Isaiah feels completely inadequate and overwhelmed (verse 5).

Isaiah 6:1–13

1 In the year that king Uzziah died [*about 740 BC*] I [*Isaiah*] saw also the Lord [*Jesus—see footnote 6c in your Bible*] sitting upon a throne, high and lifted up [*exalted*], and his train [*skirts of his robe; authority, power; Hebrew: wake, light*] filled the temple [*symbolic of heaven—see Rev. 21:22, where the celestial kingdom does not need a temple but, in effect, is a temple itself*].

2 Above it [*the throne*] stood the seraphims [*angelic beings*]: each one had six wings [*wings are symbolic of power to move and act in God's work—see D&C 77:4*]; with twain [*two*] he covered his face [*symbolic of a veil,*

which shows reverence and respect toward God in biblical culture], and with twain he covered his feet, and with twain he did fly.

3 And one cried unto another, and said, Holy, holy, holy, is the Lord of hosts [*a word repeated three times forms the superlative in Hebrew, meaning the best*]: the whole earth is full of his glory.

4 And the posts of the door moved [*shook*] at the voice of him that cried, and the house was filled with smoke [*shaking and smoke are symbolic of God's presence in biblical culture, as at Sinai, Ex. 19:18*].

Next, Isaiah tells us that he was completely overwhelmed by the experience of seeing the Savior.

5 Then said I, Woe is me! for I am undone [*completely overwhelmed*]; because I am a man of unclean lips [*I am so imperfect*], and I dwell in the midst of a people of unclean lips: for mine eyes have seen the King, the Lord of hosts.

6 Then flew one of the seraphims unto me, having a live coal [*symbolic of the Atonement; also symbolic of the Holy Ghost who guides us to the Atonement; we often say that the Holy Ghost "cleanses by fire"*] in his hand, which he had taken with the tongs from off the altar [*the altar cross, representing the Savior's sacrifice for our sins*]:

7 And he laid it [*the Atonement*] upon my mouth [*inadequacies, sins, imperfections*], and said, Lo, this [*the Atonement*] hath touched thy lips [*Isaiah's sins and*]

imperfections—see verse 5, above]; and thine iniquity is taken away, and thy sin purged [*the results of the Atonement*].

Watch now as the blessings of the Atonement give Isaiah confidence to accept his mission from the Lord. It can do the same for us in our callings.

8 Also [*then*] I heard the voice of the Lord, saying, Whom shall I send, and who will go for us? Then said I [*Isaiah*], Here am I; send me [*the cleansing power of the Atonement and help of the Spirit gave Isaiah the needed confidence to accept the call*].

Next, in verses 9–12, the Savior gives Isaiah an idea of the kinds of people he will be working with as a prophet. It will be a tough assignment. We will use a quote from Isaiah in the Book of Mormon to help with understanding verse 9.

9 And he [*the Lord*] said, Go [*this is the official call*], and tell this people, Hear ye indeed, but understand not; and see ye indeed, but perceive not.

The Book of Mormon makes significant changes to the above verse of Isaiah.

2 Nephi 16:9
9 And he said: Go and tell this people—Hear ye indeed, but they understood not; and see ye indeed, but they perceived not [*Isaiah's task will not be easy with such people*].

In verse 10, next, (which contains a chiasmus) the Lord gives Isaiah some additional insights as to the types of people he will be preaching to. In effect, the Savior appears to be telling him to imagine this in his mind's eye.

10 [*In your imagination*] Make the heart [A] of this people fat [*unfeeling, insulated from truth*], and make their ears [B] heavy [*deaf to spiritual matters*], and shut their eyes [C] [*spiritually blind*]—lest they see with their eyes [C'], and hear with their ears [B'], and understand with their heart [A'], and be converted and be healed.

There is a quote in Matthew in which the Savior basically quoted the above verse of Isaiah. Note that Matthew records that the people have refused to hear the gospel message.

Matthew 13:15
15 For this people's heart is waxed gross, and their ears are dull of hearing, and their eyes they have closed; lest at any time they should see with their eyes, and hear with their ears, and should understand with their heart, and should be converted, and I should heal them.

The Lord's description of the people with whom Isaiah would be working appears to have startled and concerned him somewhat, causing him to ask the following question:

11 Then said I, Lord, how long [*will people be like this*]? And he answered, Until the cities be wasted without

inhabitant, and the houses without man, and the land be utterly desolate [*in other words, as long as people are around*].

12 And the Lord have removed men far away [*people are gone*], and there be a great forsaking [*many deserted cities*] in the midst of the land.

In verse 13, next, Isaiah is assured that the time will never come when there are no more people, as mentioned in the scenario given in verses 11–12, above. Instead, a remnant of Israel will survive, be pruned by the Lord, and gathered.

13 But yet in it [*the land*] shall be a tenth [*a remnant*], and it [*Israel*] shall return [*includes the concept of repenting*], and shall be eaten [*in other words, pruned—as by animals eating the limbs, leaves, and branches; in other words, the Lord "prunes" his vineyard, cuts out old apostates, false doctrines, and so on; destroys old unrighteous generations so new ones may have a chance to grow*]: as a teil [*lime?*] tree, and as an oak, whose substance [*sap*] is in them, when they cast their leaves [*trees which shed the old, non-functioning leaves and look dead in winter but are still alive*]: so the holy seed shall be the substance thereof [*Israel may look dead, but there is still life in it*].

Chapter 6: Covenants

Covenants are a major part of the gospel. Perhaps you have noticed that we do not have many formal covenants and ordinances, but they are still vital for us in pursuing exaltation. Made in connection with living the gospel and keeping God's commandments, properly and sincerely made, covenants "bind" us to safe behaviors.

> Doctrine & Covenants 43:9 (emphasis added)
> 9 And thus ye shall become instructed in the law of my church, and be sanctified by that which ye have received, and ye shall **bind yourselves to act in all holiness before me**—

It is as if the Savior were inviting us to walk up to Him and tie ourselves, "bind" ourselves to Him. Making covenants is always a choice. We make these covenants in holy and peaceful settings. In such circumstances, we are more able to think clearly and make wise commitments to righteous living. Later, if we find ourselves in tempting circumstances, in turmoil and confusion, we can think of our covenants and receive strength and guidance to choose the right.

For example, when we are baptized, it is in a setting where the Spirit can bear witness to our minds and hearts that the covenant of baptism is best for us. Having been taught the gospel, we make the covenant to confirm our commitment to keep the commandments. To help us keep our baptism covenants, we are given the gift of the Holy Ghost. Then, in our lives, when we face choices between right and wrong—large or small—we can think back on what we promised at baptism and see our choices in the light of that covenant and, with the promptings of the Holy Ghost, choose the right.

When we partake of the sacrament, we renew covenants and also make covenants (listen carefully to the sacrament prayers) in a reverent environment. When we make covenants in the temple, we do so as adults, in a holy environment, where we can think rationally and clearly, feeling the presence of holy beings. We can have the Holy Ghost witness in our hearts that what we are doing is indeed wise, for us and our loved ones, and in harmony with the desires of our Father in Heaven, who wants us back home with Him and our Savior, who sacrificed all in order to enable us to gain exaltation.

Having made such covenants in settings where we can be serious-minded, we are better able to keep the commandments when tempted and our thinking processes can become cloudy and muddled. Honest people who make covenants with God are greatly strengthened by their honesty and integrity in keeping their word to God, made by covenant, when beset by Satan's tempting wiles.

Joseph, who was sold into Egyptian slavery, is a prime example of the strength brought by making commitments with the Lord to live the gospel under all circumstances. When Potiphar's wife attempts to seduce Joseph, his reply clearly shows that he has made commitments to God and is absolutely determined to keep them. Covenants and commitments made during times of peaceful introspection, accompanied by the witness of the Spirit, provide a solid foundation for wise action and self-control in times of duress and turmoil.

Genesis 39:9 (emphasis added)
9 There is none greater in this house than I; neither hath he kept back any thing from me but thee, because thou art his wife: **how then can I do this great wickedness, and sin against God?**

Perhaps you remember that Joseph's refusal of Potiphar's wife's attempts to lure him to her did not stop her from continuing her efforts. Genesis 39:10 reports that she continued "day by day" to make advances. Finally, in lustful desperation, when she found herself alone with him in the house, she grabbed at his clothes and passionately implored him to yield to her desires.

Genesis 39:12 (emphasis added)
12 And she caught him by his garment, saying, Lie with me: **and he left his garment in her hand, and fled, and got him out.**

Again, Joseph's prior commitments to God gave him the needed strength to resolutely refuse this temptation and to flee from it, regardless of what consequences it might lead to. Even as he was taken and cast in prison based on her false charges, Joseph had one of the greatest of all freedoms: freedom of conscience. And, as can be the case with us, maintaining integrity in keeping his commitments to God proved to be a great blessing in Joseph's life, despite the major setback suffered because of Potiphar's wife.

Keeping his commitments to the Lord placed Joseph in a position to constantly access the blessings of heaven, regardless of his current circumstances. Consequently, he was eventually put in charge of the prison, even though still a prisoner, and was eventually set free and became the second-in-command over all Egypt, directly under Pharaoh. In this position, he was able to save the citizens of Egypt from a terrible famine and was able to save his father and brothers and their families too. Covenants made and kept are priceless helps in daily life that also lead to eternal blessings.

Covenants Often Build upon One Another

Many years ago in an institute devotional, the General Authority speaker mentioned a common pattern in covenants we make with God. He called our students' attention to the fact that the covenants we make are often arranged in a certain order so that they build upon one another. Each strengthens and educates to prepare us for the next.

To emphasize his point, he briefly said that the covenants made in the endowment are given in a type of progression. Careful not to say things outside of the temple that would be inappropriate, he simply explained that a "progression" means that each one builds on the previous ones. It is the "line upon line, precept upon precept" principle of education in the Lord's kingdom. Isaiah explained it.

Isaiah 28:10

10 For precept must be upon precept, precept upon precept; line upon line, line upon line; here a little, and there a little:

This simple statement about the progressive nature of covenants in the gospel, particularly in the endowment, has been helpful to me throughout the years each time I have attended the temple.

The Lord used this approach in teaching Adam and Eve after they had been cast out of the Garden of Eden. We see a progression of principles as we read in Moses 5.

1. Obedience

The first step in enabling Adam and Eve to make the progress and growth intended for them throughout mortality was obedience. "Adam was obedient unto the commandments of the Lord" (Moses 5:5). See also verse 6, where Adam explains to an angel that he does not know why he is to offer sacrifices but does so out of pure obedience.

2. Sacrifice

The next element in making the full blessings of the gospel available to Adam and Eve was that of sacrifice. Sacrifice strengthens the soul. In obedience to the Lord's command, Adam built an altar and sacrificed "the first-lings of their flocks, for an offering unto the Lord" (Moses 5:5). It was a personal sacrifice, not of the "firstlings" (firstborn) of someone else's flocks or of a firstborn with blemish (see verse 5 again). They gave their finest. Obedience and sacrifice together bring out the best in those that are honest and accelerate education in the ways of God toward exaltation.

As we sacrifice things of lesser value for things of greater, as taught in the plan of salvation, we tend to grow in wisdom, perspective, and in the ability to discern where our energies and talents can best be expended.

Thus, there is a progression even here: first obedience and then sacrifice. Sacrifice based on faithful obedience opens the door for the Holy Ghost to teach, inspire, and bear witness. That is exactly what happened to Adam and Eve.

3. Knowledge of the gospel (symbolism involved in the sacrifices)

Next in this progression for Adam and Eve is a tremendous expansion of gospel knowledge. Again, we are seeing the "line upon line, precept upon precept" principle at work. Based on the foundation of obedience and sacrifice, which appears to have gone on for a considerable time

(Moses 5:6), the door is opened for a marvelous lesson about the symbolism of animal sacrifice. The central focus of the gospel, the Father's "great plan of happiness," flows to Adam and Eve from heaven as an angel teaches them. He teaches that the sacrifices Adam has been offering for "many days" are all about the future sacrifice of the "Lamb of God," the Only Begotten of the Father.

> Moses 5:7–8 (emphasis added)
>
> 7 And then the angel spake, saying: **This thing is a similitude of the sacrifice of the Only Begotten of the Father**, which is full of grace and truth.
>
> 8 Wherefore, thou shalt do all that thou doest in the name of the Son, and thou shalt repent and call upon God in the name of the Son forevermore.

The progression continues for Adam and Eve. So far we have obedience, sacrifice, and increased gospel knowledge.

And even before they enter into the covenant of baptism, the Holy Ghost will bear witness that what they have been taught is true.

4. The Holy Ghost Bears Witness and Gives Perspective

What is happening to Adam and Eve here can happen to any of us if we faithfully obey the Lord and sacrifice whatever is necessary to be loyal and consistent members of the Church. We need to listen as we are taught by authorized servants of the Lord (the angel in this case with Adam and Eve) and continue studying the gospel so that the Holy Ghost can teach us and bear testimony that it is true.

One of the great blessings of knowing it is true and still continuing to study is that the Holy Ghost becomes our teacher, such that we not only know the gospel is true, but we also know *why* it is true and why the living of the gospel brings us back to God. He, as the member of the Godhead who teaches us all things (John 14:26), helps us understand why the gospel is good for us! This is exactly what He did for Adam and Eve.

Moses 5:9–11

9 And in that day the Holy Ghost fell upon Adam, which beareth record of the Father and the Son, saying: I am the Only Begotten of the Father from the beginning, henceforth and forever, that as thou hast fallen thou mayest be redeemed, and all mankind, even as many as will.

10 And in that day Adam blessed God and was filled, and began to prophesy concerning all the families of the earth, saying: Blessed be the name of God, for because of my transgression my eyes are opened, and in this life I shall have joy, and again in the flesh I shall see God.

11 And Eve, his wife, heard all these things and was glad, saying: Were it not for our transgression we never should have had seed, and never should have known good and evil, and the joy of our redemption, and the eternal life which God giveth unto all the obedient.

Notice what happens to people, even before baptism, when the Holy Ghost comes upon them. Both Adam and Eve received great additional understanding of the plan of salvation, which led to deep appreciation and joy. This is something we can have in our days.

Next, in Moses 6, we see three additional elements of this progression, all of which involve covenants.

5. Baptism (verses 64–65)
6. Gift of the Holy Ghost (verse 66)
7. Melchizedek Priesthood for Adam (verse 67)

In summary, the pattern of making covenants that build on other covenants previously made is seen throughout the scriptures and is a prominent part of the Father's plan for us. Covenants enable us to use our agency to bind ourselves to Christ, thereby binding ourselves to safe behaviors in daily life.

Conclusion

Many years ago, on a beautiful day in June, I picked up my wife-to-be at her home and we drove to the Salt Lake Temple. It was our wedding day. After dressing in our temple clothing, we were escorted by friendly "human" angels to one of the magnificent sealing rooms in the Salt Lake Temple, where family and loved ones waited to greet us. The Spirit was strong and bore testimony that we were in the right place, doing the right thing. It was indescribable! After waiting a few minutes, Elder Harold B. Lee, of the Quorum of the Twelve, entered the room. His was a commanding but pleasant presence. He greeted us and all present, and then spent several minutes giving us inspired counsel. I remember the feeling that he was receiving direct revelation as he addressed us. It was personal and beautiful.

Soon, he invited us to kneel at the altar and then, by the power of the Melchizedek Priesthood, he sealed us as husband and wife for time and all eternity. I can still see that powerful and tranquil scene in my mind's eye. I can still feel the Spirit surrounding us. The Holy Ghost still bears witness to my heart and soul as to the validity and power of that ordinance in the temple of God. On that special day, we were organized into our own eternal family unit by a servant of the Lord who held the power and authority to do so. Such is the glory of temples to join heaven with earth, bringing eternal family blessings to the Father's children.

Thoughts on Temple Experiences

_____

_____

_____

_____

_____

_____

_____

_____

_____

_____

_____

_____

_____

_____

_____

_____

_____

_____

_____

_____

_____

_____

_____

_____

_____

_____

_____

_____

_____

_____

_____

_____

_____

_____

_____

_____

_____

_____

_____

_____

_____

_____

_____

_____

_____

_____

_____

_____

_____

_____

_____

_____

_____

_____

_____

_____

_____

_____

_____

_____

_____

_____

_____

_____

_____

_____

_____

_____

_____

_____

About the Author

David J. Ridges taught for the Church Educational System for thirty-five years and for several years at BYU Campus Education Week. He taught adult religion classes and Know Your Religion classes for BYU Continuing Education for many years. He has also served as a curriculum writer for Sunday School, seminary, and institute of religion manuals.

He has served in many callings in the Church, including Gospel Doctrine teacher, bishop, stake president, and patriarch.

He and Sister Ridges have served two full-time CES missions together. They are the parents of six children and grandparents of eleven grandchildren so far. They make their home in Springville, Utah.